Childcraft
The How and Why Library

Volume 14

About Me

World Book, Inc.

a Scott Fetzer company

Chicago London Sydney Toronto

Acknowledgments

The publishers of *Childcraft—The How and Why Library*
gratefully acknowledge the courtesy of the following
publishers and organizations. Full illustration
acknowledgments for this volume appear on pages
281-282.

Central School, Glencoe Public Schools, Glencoe,
Ill.: Selections from *Golden Treasury of Stories*
Publication #1.

Kenmore-Town of Tonawanda Public Schools, Kenmore,
N.Y.: Selections from *Wisdom Comes Dancing,* 1967.

Oakland Elementary Schools, Oakland, Calif.: Selections
from *Calliope,* compiled by Virginia M. Reid.

Racine Unified School District, No. 1, Racine, Wis.:
Selections from *Racine Writings, 1966-1968.*

Richardson Independent School District, Richardson, Tex.:
Selections from *Imagination '66* and *Imagination '67.*

Riverside Elementary Schools, Riverside, Ill.: Selections
from *R.G.S. 1968.*

San Diego City Schools, San Diego, Calif.: Selections
from *Impressions,* 1967, and *Impressions,* 1968.

Simon & Schuster, Inc.: "My Feelings" by Paul
Thompson, "My Uncle Jack" by David Amey, and
"Thunder" by Glenys Van Every from *Miracles,* edited
by Richard Lewis, © 1966 by Richard Lewis. Reprinted by
permission of Simon & Schuster and Penguin Books, Ltd.

Year Book Medical Publishers: X-ray photographs
on page 157 from *Growth and Development of
Children* by E. H. Watson and G. H. Lowrey © 1967
Year Book Medical Publishers.

Volume 14

About Me

Contents

What Does <u>Me</u> Mean to Me?

There are millions of
people in the world.
Many are grown-ups.
But a great many
are children.
Some are boys.
Some are girls.
Boys . . . girls . . .
big or small . . .
thin or fat . . .
short or tall.

All call themselves "Me."

Everyone is a "me"

Each person in my family is a "me." Every one of my friends is a "me."

Of course, all those "me's" are people. So they are all alike in many ways.

All people have human bodies.

All people come into the world in the same way.

All people have someone, or a few very special people, they love.

All people laugh and cry, feel happy and sad and angry and afraid, do good things and bad things and brave things and kind things.

And all people explore their world and learn about it.

People are special

People are very special. They do lots of very special things.

They make many different kinds of foods to eat, clothes to wear, and places to live in.

They make all kinds of tools to use in their work.

They make things that have many parts in them—cars, television sets, spaceships, computers.

They play all kinds of indoor and outdoor games.

They make all kinds of toys—from cuddly teddy bears to high-flying kites.

They make statues, paintings, gardens, and buildings that are beautiful to look at.

They write wonderful stories, poems, and songs to read and to listen to.

They can imagine things they have never seen and places they have never been.

They can ask questions.

And they can wonder.

A sense of wonder

Boys and girls everywhere wonder about the things they see around them. And they wonder about themselves, too.

They wonder how their bodies work.

They wonder about their secret selves—their thoughts and wishes and the way they feel about things.

They wonder if they are like everyone else.

They wonder how they are different.

They look for answers. And sometimes they find answers in books like this one.

And so, this book was made for <u>me</u>—because I am someone very special, and because I wonder about things.

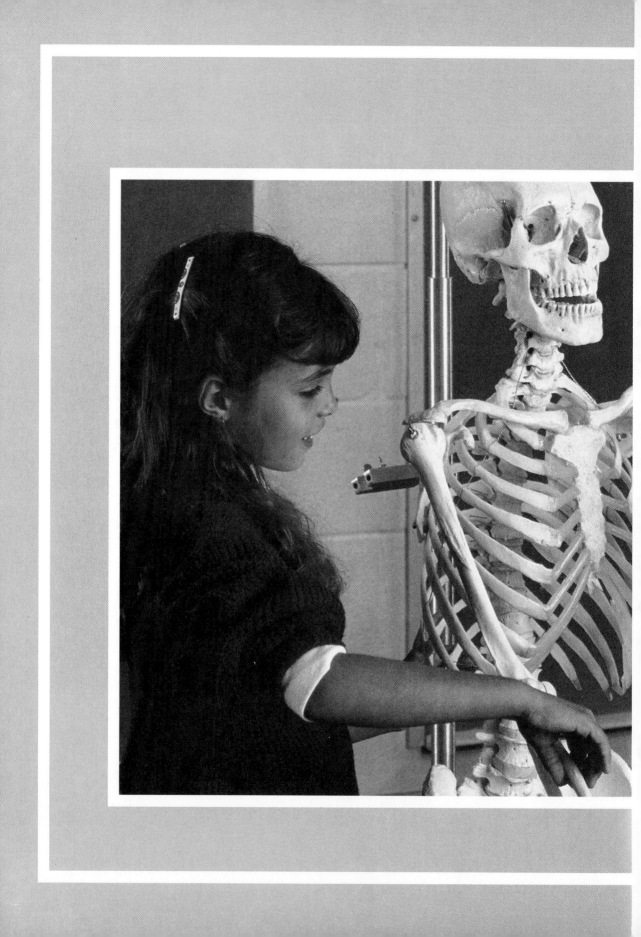

Inside and Outside of Me

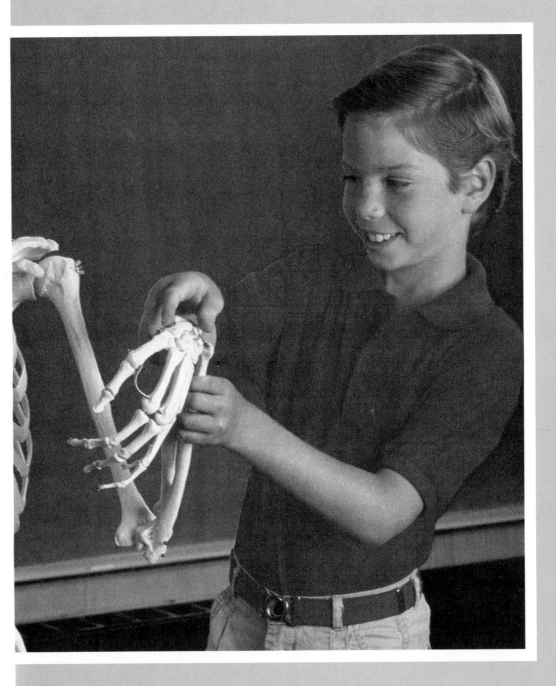

The me that I can see

It's fun to watch myself in a mirror. A mirror shows me what I look like. A mirror helps me learn about myself.

It's fun to play in front of a mirror. I can make up a poem about that:

In the mirror I can see
A copycat who plays with me.
I wrinkle my nose and he does, too.
His mouth gets round when I say, "Boo!"
I waggle my tongue like this and that.
And so does he, that copycat.
He has my teeth, my ears, my eyes,
And everything is just my size.
Who is that copycat I see?
That copycat I see is me!

I laugh at the faces I make in front of a mirror. But if I'm trying to learn about myself, it's better to look very hard at myself as I really am. I see my face.

I see my face

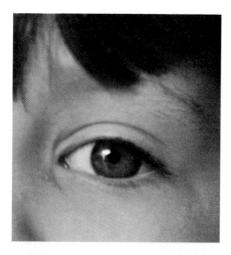

I see my eyes. There are eyebrows above them and eyelashes around them. My eyelashes and eyebrows keep dust and dirt out of my eyes.

I look closely at one of my eyes. The colored circle is my iris. Irises can be blue, brown, green, or gray. The dark dot in the center of my iris is my pupil. The pupil is a round doorway to the inside of my eye.

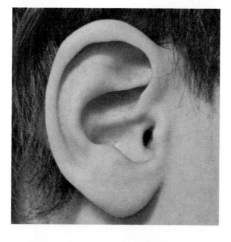

I see my ears. My ears are soundcatchers. Little tunnels in my ears lead to the inside of my head. The sounds I hear enter my head through these tunnels.

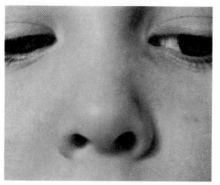

I see my nose. My nose has two holes in it. The air I breathe and the smells I smell go in through the holes.

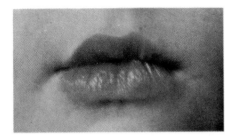

I see my mouth. My mouth leads to the inside of my body. I use my mouth for eating, drinking, and talking. Sometimes I breathe through my mouth, too.

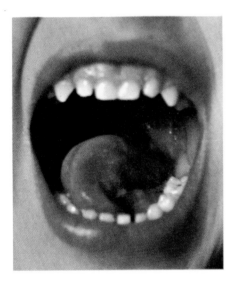

I see my tongue. It keeps busy. I talk and it helps me say words. I chew and it moves my food. Little bumps on my tongue help me taste my food.

I see my teeth. My front teeth are sharp. They cut my food. The rest of my teeth grind and mash my food. When I talk, my tongue, lips, and teeth help me make the right sounds.

My hair

About a hundred thousand hairs cover the top of my head. I can pull out a hair and a new one will grow to take its place. The hair grows and is cut and grows some more. Where does all that hair come from?

Each hair grows out of a tiny hole in my skin. At the bottom of each hole are tiny veins and arteries. They bring blood to the root of the hair. The hair takes food and oxygen from the blood. This makes the hair grow.

Around each hair is a little pocket of oil. The oil makes my hair shine.

Each tiny hole has a muscle, too. If I'm scared I may say that my hair stands on end. It doesn't—it just feels that way! What I'm feeling are the tiny muscles moving the skin on the top of my head.

Some hair is straight. Some is curly. A straight hair is like a round toothpick. A curly hair is round, but it has little flat places in it. I can feel this by rolling a straight hair and a curly hair between my fingers. The straight hair rolls smoothly, but the curly hair feels more rough between my fingers.

Some hair doesn't grow long. Eyelashes and eyebrows never grow very much. But the hair on my head can grow as much as six inches (15 centimeters) a year.

A hair follicle

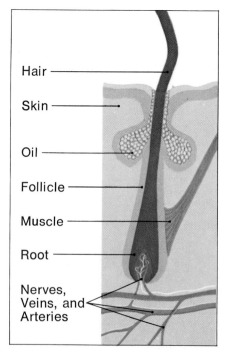

Hair

Skin

Oil

Follicle

Muscle

Root

Nerves, Veins, and Arteries

Mike's hair is red.

Black hair covers Zuki's head.

Jane's hair is brown.

Blond hair grows on Peter's crown.

Skin can be light
or dark.

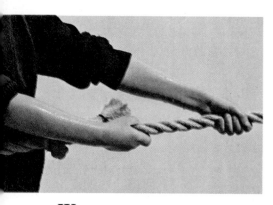

When I'm hot, I sweat.

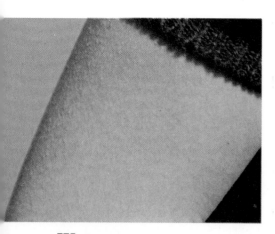

When I'm cold, I get
"goosebumps."

My skin covers me

My skin is tough. I scratch it and scrub it and scrape it and rub it. Sometimes I bruise it or cut it. But it always grows back.

Tiny bits of color are in my skin. They make my skin black or brown or red or yellow or white or freckled.

The color in my skin helps protect me from sunburn. The sun's rays don't pass through the bits of color very well.

My skin does more than just cover me. It helps to cool me and it helps to warm me.

Tiny holes called pores are in my skin. When I'm hot, drops of sweat come out through the pores. As the sweat dries, I feel cooler.

When I'm cold, my pores close and no sweat gets out. Sometimes when I'm cold I shiver. Shivering helps to warm me. It is caused by tiny muscles moving in my skin.

If I get cold suddenly, the tiny muscles tighten. You might almost say my skin shrinks. When that happens, the hairs on my body stand up straight and their follicles make little bumps under my skin. I call the bumps "goosebumps."

My navel

In the middle of my belly is a mark. It is my navel. Sometimes I call it my "belly-button." I used to wonder why it was there. Now I know.

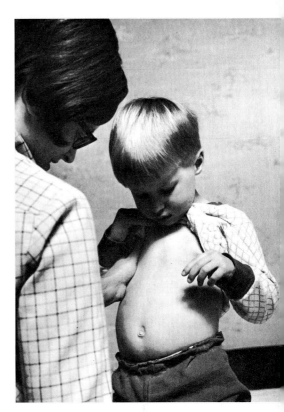

In the months before I was born, I lived inside my mother. I was joined to her by a kind of tube called the umbilical cord. The cord was joined to me in the middle of my belly. Through it, I received the food and oxygen I needed to live and grow. Through it, wastes left my body.

For nine months I lived and grew because this cord joined me to my mother.

When I was big enough to live by myself I left my mother's body. I was born.

Now I could drink milk.

Now my kidneys and intestines could get rid of wastes for me.

Now I could breathe with my lungs.

I didn't need the umbilical cord anymore. The doctor cut the cord right after I was born. In a week or so, all that was left was the "button" in the middle of my belly, my navel.

How I move

When I was a baby, I couldn't walk. I couldn't pick up anything. As I grew, I learned to make my hands and arms and feet and legs work for me.

Now I use my legs for many jobs. I use them to walk, skip, jump, run, stoop, and climb. My legs can bend because they have joints, places that move like the hinges on a door. If my legs had no knee joints, I wouldn't be able to move well. As a game, I keep my legs stiff and try to sit down and stand up.

My arms have joints, too. I use my arms to carry, push, pull, lift, throw, and do many other jobs. But if I hold my arms out straight and pretend that I have no elbow joints, I can't even feed myself.

How big am I now?

Am I short?

I'm shorter than my father. My father is shorter than a camel. A camel is shorter than a giraffe. I'm shorter than a man, a camel, and a giraffe.

Am I tall?

I'm taller than a lamb. A lamb is taller than a chicken. A chicken is taller than a mouse. I'm taller than a lamb, a chicken, and a mouse.

Am I small?

I'm smaller than a horse. A horse is smaller than an elephant. An elephant is smaller than a whale. I'm smaller than a horse, an elephant, and a whale.

Am I big?

I'm bigger than a cat. A cat is bigger than a robin. A robin is bigger than a bee. I'm bigger than a cat, a robin, and a bee.

I'm just the right size for me!

My hands and feet

My hands and feet are important parts of me that I can see. I use them to do all kinds of work.

My fingers and thumbs pick up things and hold them. When I try to pick up things without using my thumb, my fingers don't work well.

My fingers and thumbs are good tools. I use them to button my coat, tie the laces on my sneakers, turn a doorknob, hold my chopsticks when I eat, and other jobs.

My fingers touch and feel things. They help me know when something is hot or cold, soft or hard, smooth, rough, or prickly.

I use my hands to protect myself. If I get into a fight, I can make my hands into fists to defend myself. I can use my hands to shield my eyes from bright

lights or to brush away a fly. My hands are especially good for holding a kitten or fixing my hair.

My feet can do some of the things my hands can do. I can use my feet to touch and feel things. And if I try hard, I can even pick up things and hold them with my toes. My toes can't do these things nearly as well as my fingers. But my toes help me to jump when I play hopscotch or skip rope.

My feet can do things my hands can't do. My feet support the weight of all the rest of my body so that I can stand, walk, run, jump, and go whizzing along on my roller skates.

I can stand on my hands, and even walk on them for a short distance. But my feet are better at this job than my hands are. My feet are especially good for dancing, kicking a football, and playing soccer.

The outside of me

My skin is one of the organs of my body. Some waste products are carried out of my body through my skin when I sweat. And my skin helps keep my body at an even temperature.

All skin is tough, but some parts are tougher than others. The skin on the bottoms of my feet is toughest of all.

Some of my skin is quite thick and some is quite thin. The thickest skin is on my back. The thinnest skin is on my eyelids.

All skin, even the thinnest, is made up of two layers. The outer layer is called the epidermis. The inner layer is called the dermis.

All skin, even the thinnest, contains tiny veins and arteries filled with blood; nerves that help me feel heat, cold, or pain; and glands that give out sweat and oil. Some parts of my skin also contain hair. Hair grows out of little holes called follicles.

I can see my skin. But I can't see all the things that are under it. I can't see the muscles and bones and nerves and the many organs that keep my body working for me.

Since I can't see these things, I'll look at pictures of them.

My muscles

My body is filled with muscles.

Deep inside of me, muscles help my body work properly. Muscles help food move through my body. And muscles help air move in and out of my lungs.

Some of my muscles are fastened to my bones, and these muscles help me move.

Muscles work in groups. In my arms, the biceps and the triceps muscles work together. If I bend my arm, I can feel the biceps in my upper arm.

Some muscles that must do big jobs are joined to my bones by strong, tough cords called tendons. I can feel tendons on the insides of my wrists and at the backs of my ankles. The tendon in my ankle is called the Achilles' tendon. It joins my calf muscles to my heel.

My chest muscles help me breathe.

My leg muscles help me run and skip.

My arm muscles help me lift and carry things.

My neck muscles help me hold up my head.

The muscles in my face help me wink and smile and make a funny face.

In the pictures, some muscles can be seen in the boy's body that cannot be seen in the girl's. They can be seen in the boy because his body is turned.

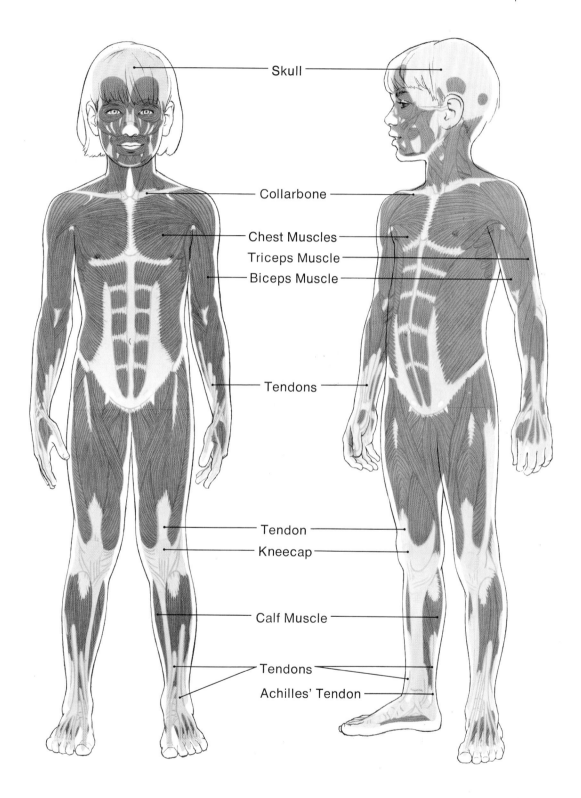

Skull

Collarbone

Chest Muscles

Triceps Muscle

Biceps Muscle

Tendons

Tendon

Kneecap

Calf Muscle

Tendons

Achilles' Tendon

My bones

My skeleton grows up with me. When I am grown, I will have about 206 bones.

Bones give shape to my body.

Bones store up minerals to be used as my body needs them.

New blood cells are made inside my bones.

Bones protect my inner organs. The bones in my skull protect my brain. The bones in my spine protect my spinal cord. The bones in my chest protect my heart and lungs.

There is cartilage between most of my bones. Cartilage is softer than bone. It keeps bones from rubbing against each other.

Bones fit together at places called joints. Some joints, such as those in my skull, do not move. Other joints, like those in my legs, do move. Only a few joints are named in the picture. I have other joints in my jaws, shoulders, hips, wrists, ankles, fingers, and toes.

My bones work together in groups, and so I am able to move around.

In the pictures, some bones can be seen in the boy's body that cannot be seen in the girl's. They can be seen in the boy because his body is turned.

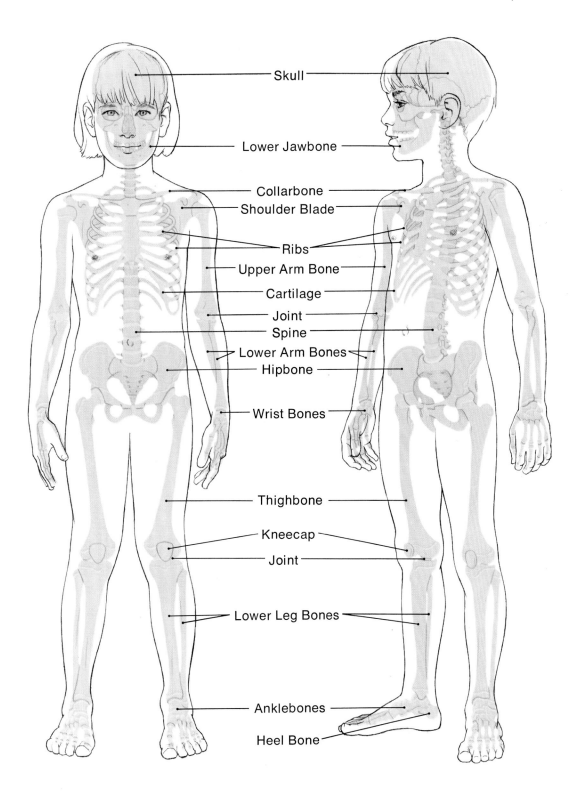

Skull

Lower Jawbone

Collarbone
Shoulder Blade

Ribs

Upper Arm Bone

Cartilage

Joint

Spine

Lower Arm Bones

Hipbone

Wrist Bones

Thighbone

Kneecap

Joint

Lower Leg Bones

Anklebones

Heel Bone

I breathe

I breathe in and out through my nose and mouth.

Fresh air is made warm and clean in my nasal cavity.

The air goes down my trachea, through my bronchial tubes, and deep into my two lungs.

Used air leaves my lungs through my bronchial tubes. It goes up my trachea and leaves my body through my nose and mouth.

My nasal cavity and my sinuses are in my head. My trachea is in my throat. My lungs are in my chest.

Under my lungs is a big, strong muscle. It is called my diaphragm. My diaphragm helps my lungs pull in fresh air and push out used air.

Around my lungs are 24 ribs and many muscles. My ribs and muscles protect my lungs and help my lungs move in and out.

In the pictures on the next page, some things can be seen in the boy's body which cannot be seen in the girl's. They can be seen in the boy because his body is turned.

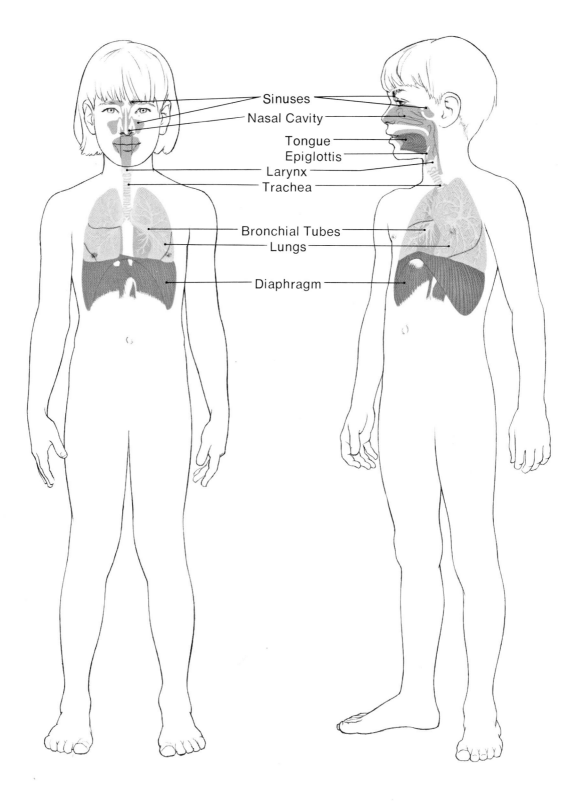

Sinuses
Nasal Cavity
Tongue
Epiglottis
Larynx
Trachea
Bronchial Tubes
Lungs
Diaphragm

My heart and blood

My heart is about as big as my fist. Each side of it works.

The right side receives blood from the rest of my body. It pumps the blood to my lungs. In my lungs, blood takes oxygen from the air.

The left side of my heart receives fresh blood from my lungs. It pumps the blood back through my body.

Arteries carry fresh blood from my heart to all the parts of my body. But the arteries from my heart to my lungs carry used blood. On the next page, arteries are red except for the arteries between the lungs and heart.

Veins carry used blood from all the parts of my body to my heart. But the veins from my lungs to my heart carry fresh blood. On the next page, veins are blue except for the veins between the lungs and heart.

The doctor can take my pulse to find out how fast my heart is beating. My pulse shows how fast the blood is being pushed through the artery in my wrist.

Boys and girls have exactly the same kinds of veins and arteries. In the picture, the girl shows what they look like and the boy shows how they work.

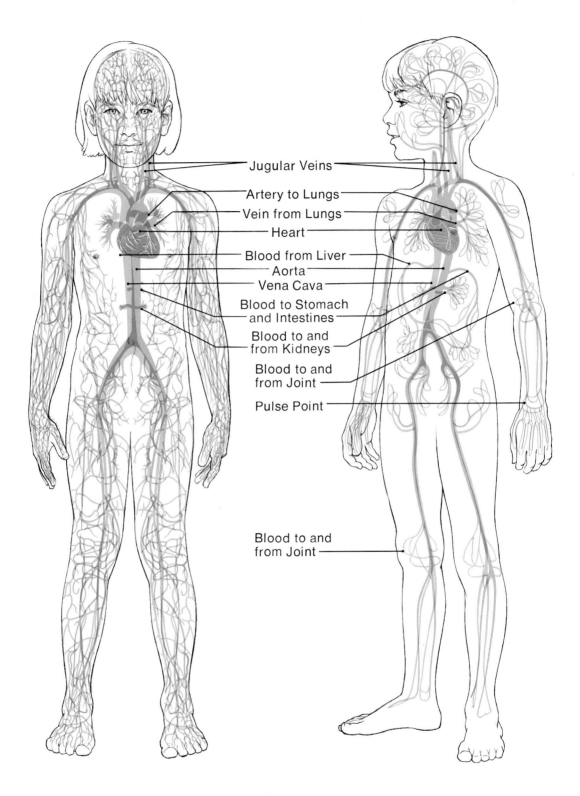

Jugular Veins

Artery to Lungs

Vein from Lungs

Heart

Blood from Liver

Aorta

Vena Cava

Blood to Stomach
and Intestines

Blood to and
from Kidneys

Blood to and
from Joint

Pulse Point

Blood to and
from Joint

I eat food

I use my tongue and teeth when I eat. These help me grind up and mix my food.

I use muscles, too, when I eat. I use muscles in my jaws, throat, esophagus, stomach, and intestines.

Special organs and glands in my body make liquids that help me digest food.

Glands in my mouth make saliva, which I mix with food. Glands in my stomach and small intestine add other liquids. The most important part of digestion happens in my small intestine.

My pancreas sends liquid to my small intestine. So does my liver. My liver lies just under my diaphragm.

In the pictures on the next page, some things can be seen in the boy's body which are hidden in the girl's body. The boy and girl have the same organs for digesting food. But the boy's stomach, liver, and intestines have been made smaller in the picture so that the other organs can be seen.

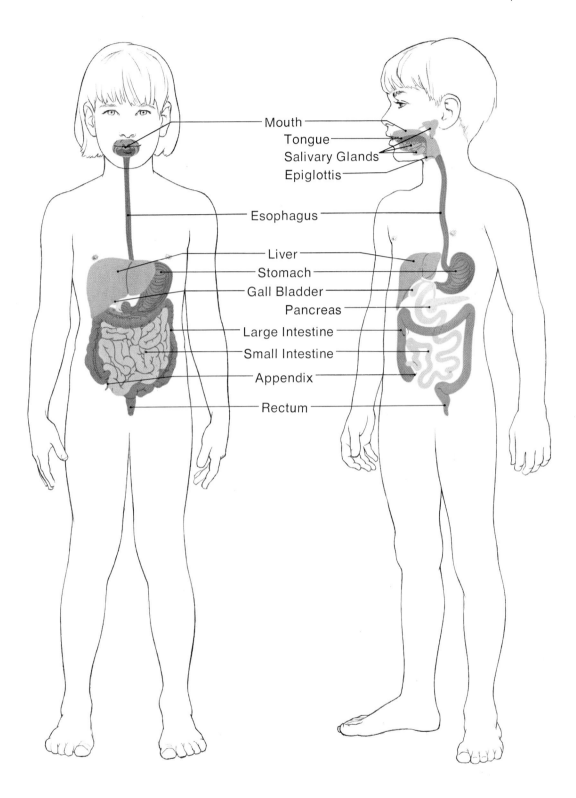

Mouth
Tongue
Salivary Glands
Epiglottis

Esophagus

Liver
Stomach
Gall Bladder
Pancreas
Large Intestine
Small Intestine
Appendix
Rectum

My kidneys and other organs

In my back, just below my ribs, on each side of my spine, are my kidneys. My kidneys are about half as big as my heart. They are shaped like beans.

Kidneys do an important job for my body—they help keep my blood clean.

My blood takes waste products, things my body cannot use, away from my cells. My blood passes through my kidneys, and my kidneys take the waste products out of my blood.

The liquid from my kidneys is called urine. Urine leaves my kidneys through two tubes called ureters. The urine goes into my bladder. From there, it leaves my body through another tube called the urethra.

Also shown in the pictures are some of the organs girls or boys will need when they grow up and wish to become mothers and fathers. In the girl, these organs are the ovaries, the uterus, and the vagina. In the boy, these organs are the testicles.

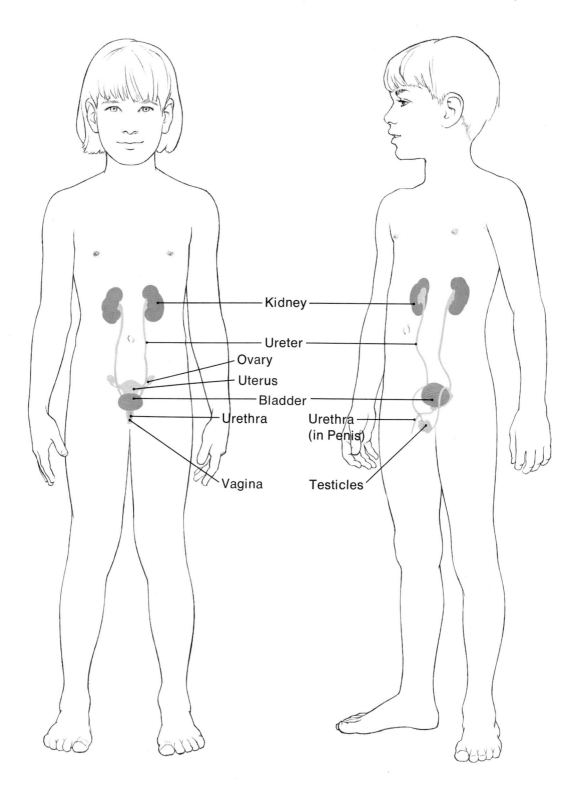

Kidney

Ureter

Ovary

Uterus

Bladder

Urethra

Urethra
(in Penis)

Vagina

Testicles

My body's control center

My brain is the control center of my body. I have one brain. It is in my skull.

My spinal cord is the path along which most messages move to and from my brain. I have one spinal cord. It is in my spine.

Nerves lead from my muscles and organs to my spinal cord. There are many thousands of nerves all over my body.

My nerves carry messages from my brain to my arms and legs, fingers and toes, and so I am able to move.

My nerves also carry messages about heat and cold and pain to my brain.

I know when I am using some nerves. Other nerves are always at work even though I don't know it. They carry messages between my brain and my heart, lungs, stomach, intestines, and other organs. My brain keeps these organs working all the time. Even if I tried to stop my heart or lungs, I could not.

Special nerves carry information from my eyes, ears, nose, and mouth to my brain. My brain tells me about them.

Boys and girls have the same kinds of nerves in their bodies. In the picture, some are shown in the girl and some in the boy so they can be seen more clearly.

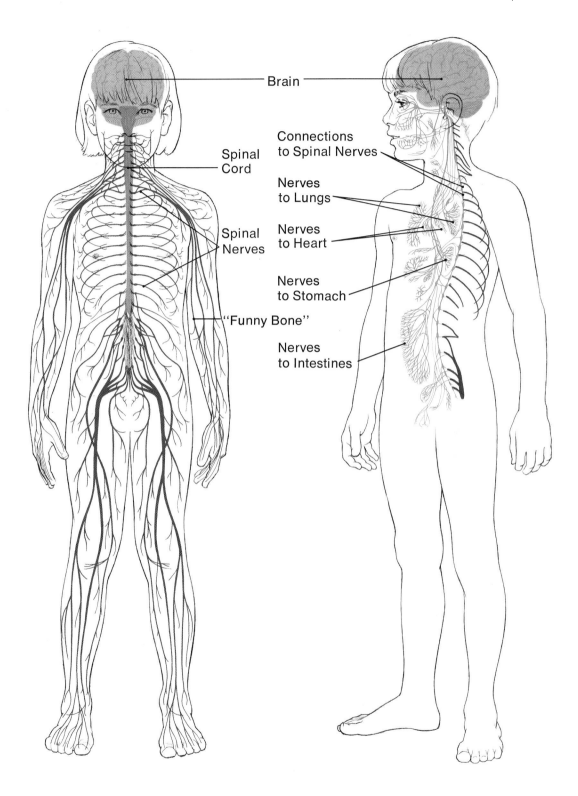

Brain

Spinal
Cord

Connections
to Spinal Nerves

Nerves
to Lungs

Spinal
Nerves

Nerves
to Heart

Nerves
to Stomach

"Funny Bone"

Nerves
to Intestines

What is a cell?

All living things—plants, animals, and people—are made of cells. I am made of cells.

A cell is the smallest living part of me it is possible to imagine. A cell can be long, short, thin, fat, square, or round. It is made of a soft jellylike material called protoplasm. A cell is so small it can be seen only through a microscope.

All cells grow and divide. Every minute my body makes more than a billion new cells. Cells make new cells by growing and splitting in two.

In order to live, cells need food and oxygen. Oxygen is in the air. I breathe air. I eat food. My body changes these a little bit, and then my blood is able to carry them to all the cells in my body.

My cells use up the food and oxygen and give off things cells cannot use. The useless things are called waste products. My blood carries waste products away from my cells.

Cells do special jobs. I have skin cells, bone cells, blood cells, brain cells. All together, billions of cells make up the body of the person I call "Me."

A skin cell

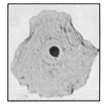

Some of the cells in my body are bigger than others. But all are tiny. About 6 million skin cells would fit into the empty square.

My fingernails and toenails

My fingernails and toenails are made up of hard skin cells. These cells are formed by the same protein that makes my hair strong. Animals' claws and hoofs are made of the same thing.

My nails grow from the base, where I see a pale shape that looks like part of the moon. It's pale because the cells there are smaller than the other cells in the skin under my nails. The outer skin at the base of my nails is known as my cuticle.

My nails grow all the time. If I make a mud pie, or play with sand, dirt gets under the tips of my fingernails. So I scrub them and clip them to keep them clean. I clip my toenails straight across so they won't grow back into the flesh at the corners of my toes.

Why do I have nails? To protect the ends of my fingers and toes!

Fingernails

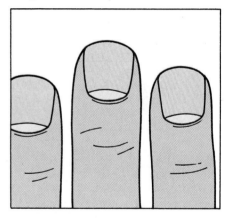

Toenails

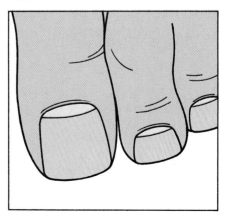

When I look at a model of a human body, I can see what's inside my body.

The me that I can't see

What does the inside of me look like? What's inside my finger, my head, my chest? I know many of the things that are in there.

I have bones. I touch my fingers and toes and feel the bones. I feel bones when I touch my ribs or head or elbows.

I have muscles. I touch the upper part of my arms and feel the muscles. When I eat, I touch my jaws and feel the muscles that help me chew.

I have blood. I've seen my blood. Once I cut myself and some blood came out.

I have lungs. I feel my chest move in and out when I breathe. That means my lungs are working.

I have a heart. When I put my hand on my chest, I feel a thumping. That's my heart beating.

I have tonsils. I can see part of my tonsils if I open my mouth, stick out my tongue, and look in a mirror. My tonsils are at the back of my mouth, on each side.

I have a stomach. If my stomach is empty, it may rumble. If I fill it too full, I may have a stomach-ache.

I have a brain. I use my brain to think. And my brain helps me know what I see, taste, smell, hear, and touch.

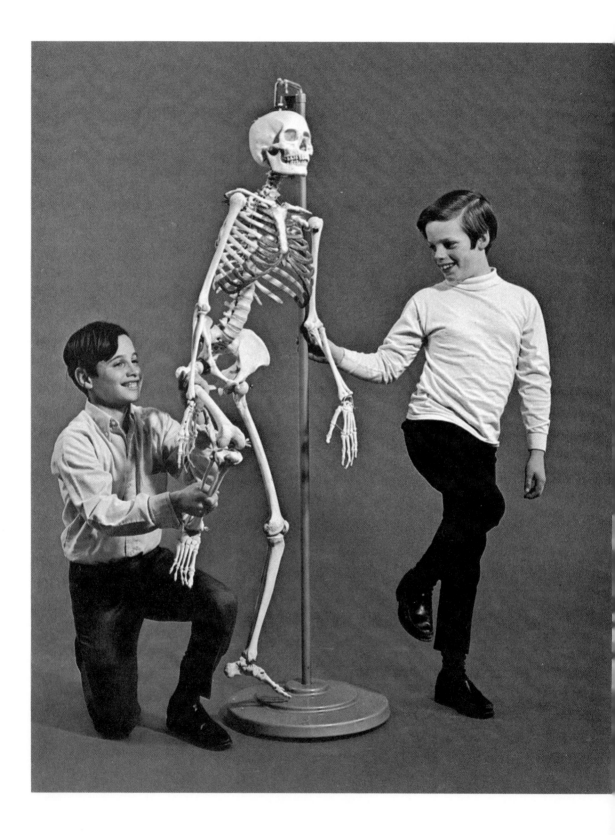

My body's framework

I have a skeleton inside of me. That's what my bones are called. If I had no bones, I wouldn't be able to stand or bend or run or play. I'd be floppy like a rag doll.

I have bones of many shapes and sizes. Leg bones are long. Toe bones are short. Rib bones are rounded. Some bones in my head are flat. The bones in my spine look a little like the spools that hold thread.

Some bones, like those in the top of my head, can't move. Others, like those in my legs, fit together so that they do move. That's why I can bend and move so well.

My bones are hard. But they are not so hard on the inside as they are on the outside. Inside, the bone cells are not so tightly packed together and there are many tiny holes between the cells.

Some bones, like those in my legs, are hollow like tubes. Inside the hollow is bone marrow. Marrow is made up of tissue, fat, tiny veins and arteries, and cells that make new blood cells for my body.

Every day new cells are added to my bones, and my bones become longer and larger.

My fingers

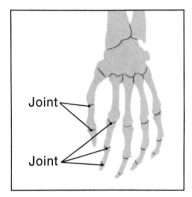

My fingers bend

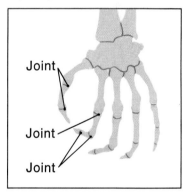

These are some of the joints I use when I hold something between my thumb and first finger.

Muscles help me move

I can move because I have muscles. Muscles that help me move are fastened to my bones and are elastic, like rubber bands. They can stretch out and draw back together again.

Some muscles, like the big ones in my arms and legs, have strong cords called tendons at their ends. The muscles are fastened to my bones by these tendons.

Muscles work together in groups. As some of them tighten and become shorter, the other muscles in the group get longer. That's what happens when I bend my elbow or knee and straighten it again. If I had no muscles, I wouldn't be able to move or even stand.

My body has more than 600 major muscles. Besides those that help me move, others help to keep my body working. These are not fastened to my bones.

Muscles in my stomach and intestines mix and mash my food. Muscles in my chest help me breathe. And my heart is a very special kind of extra-strong muscle.

My arm muscles

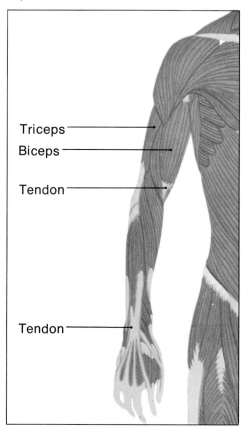

Triceps
Biceps
Tendon
Tendon

Muscles help me bend my arm or straighten it. The muscle in the front of my arm is my biceps. The muscle in the back of my arm is my triceps. My biceps and my triceps work together.

Muscles work together

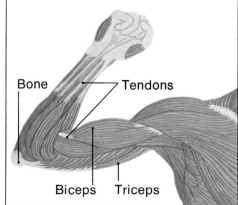

Bone
Tendons
Biceps
Triceps

Air for my body

When I breathe, air enters my nose. The inside of my nose warms the air. Little hairs in my nose catch the dust in the air. The wetness in my nose catches most of the germs I breathe in.

The warm, clean air goes down a tube called the trachea, and into my lungs. I can feel my trachea in the front of my throat.

My lungs are in my chest. My ribs make a kind of cage around my lungs that protects them.

Below my lungs is a strong muscle called the diaphragm. My diaphragm and the muscles fastened to my ribs move my chest in and out, in and out. When my chest moves out, fresh air comes into my lungs. When my chest moves in, used air leaves my lungs. My muscles and bones help me breathe.

The air I breathe in has oxygen in it. Oxygen is a gas. I can't see, taste, feel, or smell oxygen. But my body needs it to live.

The air I breathe out has carbon dioxide in it. My body makes more carbon dioxide than it needs. I breathe out the extra carbon dioxide.

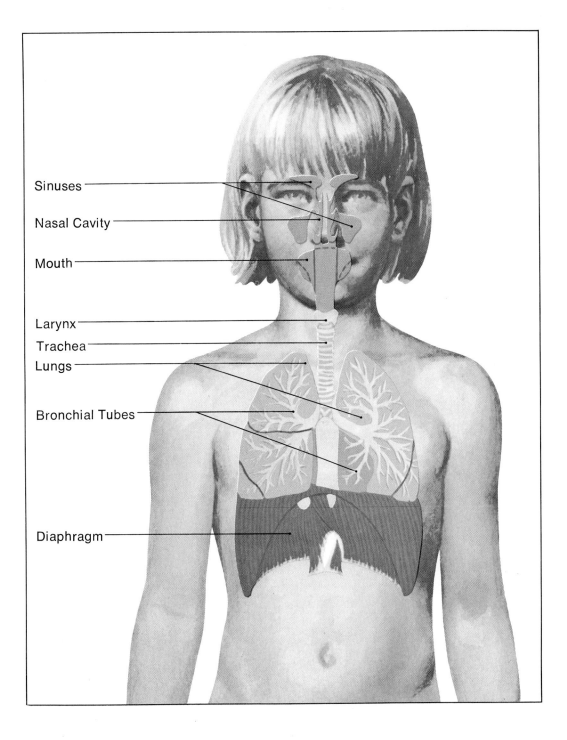

Sinuses

Nasal Cavity

Mouth

Larynx

Trachea

Lungs

Bronchial Tubes

Diaphragm

My heart pumps blood

Blood moves fast. And my heart is what makes it move. Blood leaving my heart right now will travel all the way to my toes and back again in about one minute.

Inside my body are thousands of tubes called arteries and veins. My heart pumps blood through these tubes to all the parts of my body. That's what my heart is doing when I put my hand on my chest and feel a thumping.

Blood flows away from my heart through my arteries. The blood is fresh. It carries oxygen from my lungs to all the cells of my body.

Blood flows back to my heart through my veins. This blood is not fresh. It has given up its oxygen. Now it carries carbon dioxide from all the cells in my body.

My heart pumps the used blood through my lungs. There the blood trades the carbon dioxide for oxygen. Then my heart pumps the fresh blood into my arteries and back through my body.

Blood has red cells in it. The red cells are workers. They carry oxygen and carbon dioxide.

Blood has white cells in it, too. These are fighters. They kill germs and help me stay strong and healthy.

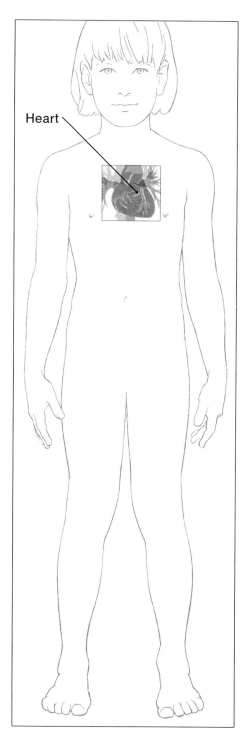

Heart

Blood flows through my heart

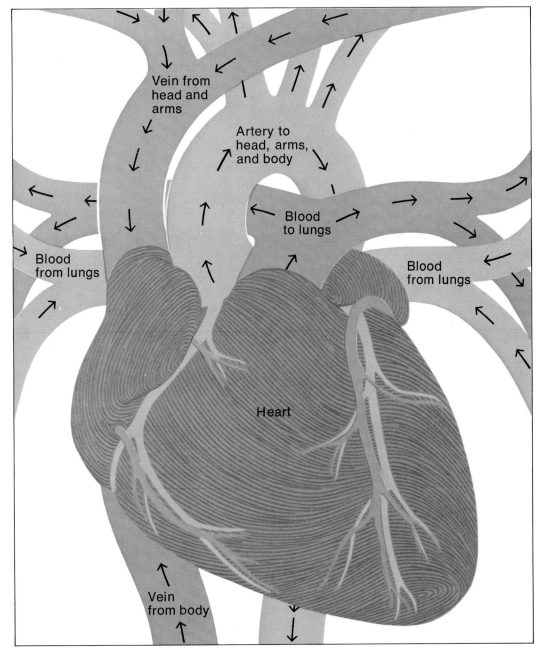

Blood flows away from my heart through
my arteries. Blood flows back to my
heart through my veins.

Blood moves through my body

My blood carries oxygen to my cells.

Every cell in my body needs oxygen in order to live. Bone cells, muscle cells, brain cells—all must have oxygen.

Every cell in my body gives off things my body cannot use, called wastes. Bone cells, muscle cells, brain cells—all give off waste materials.

My blood carries waste materials away from my cells. The waste materials must be cleaned out of my blood. That happens as the blood passes through my kidneys. My kidneys are behind my stomach near my spine.

The waste materials make a liquid in my kidneys. This liquid is called urine. The urine flows down long tubes into my bladder. Another tube leads from my bladder outside my body. Urine passes through this tube, the urethra.

My body has between two and four quarts (2 and 4 liters) of blood. If I cut myself and lose some, my body makes new blood to take its place.

Blood cells are made inside my bones. New ones are made every second. In less time than it takes to count to two hundred, my bones can make more than 100 million new cells for my blood.

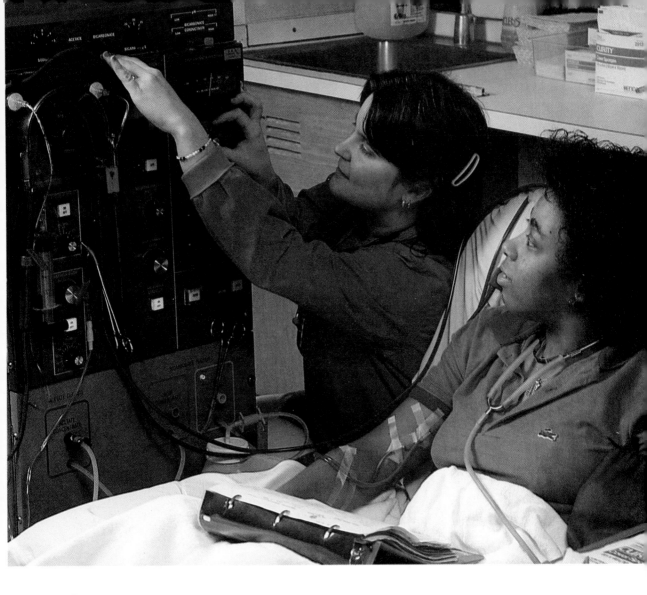

This machine takes the place of a
person's kidneys. When someone's
kidneys do not work as they
should, the machine cleans waste
products from the person's blood.

Some foods help my body grow and grow.

Some foods help my
body stay warm.

Some foods help my
body work properly.

Food to grow on

Sometimes I don't wear out my shoes —I grow out of them. My baby shoes are much, much too small for me now. But Dad's shoes are much, much too big. I wonder how big my feet will grow to be.

My feet and I are bigger than we were last year. And, my feet and I will be even bigger next year. That's because I am growing. Food helps me to grow.

I keep warm. No matter how cold the day, my body stays comfortably warm inside. It takes food to keep me warm.

All the parts of my body work together as a group. My body needs food to work smoothly.

Some foods help me grow.

Some foods help me stay warm.

Some foods help my body work properly.

I don't have to tell my body which food is which. I just swallow the food, and my body digests it and uses it as it is needed.

But how does all that happen? How do hamburgers and beans and tomatoes and milk and bread and apples turn into the kinds of things my body can use?

This is how it happens.

I chew and swallow

Suppose I've been playing hard and I'm very hungry. Lunch tastes good. But as good as the food is, my body can't use it without changing it. The changing is called digestion. The most important part of digestion happens inside of me, in my small intestine. But some changes happen as soon as I put food into my mouth.

My teeth cut and grind the food into many small pieces. My tongue mixes it

My body uses proteins to build new cells. Meat, cheese, milk, eggs, and other foods have protein in them.

with the saliva in my mouth. The food becomes wet and easy to swallow. Then my tongue pushes it to the back of my mouth.

I don't swallow the food until I'm ready. But once I have swallowed it, it is on its way through my body. I don't have to think about digesting the food. My body changes the food and uses it as it is needed—to help me grow, to keep me warm, and to keep my body running smoothly.

My body uses carbohydrates and fats to keep me warm. Sugar has carbohydrate in it. So does flour. Meat, eggs, and other foods contain fat.

My body needs vitamins and minerals to run smoothly. Fruits, vegetables, cereals, and other foods have vitamins and minerals in them.

What happens to my food?

I swallow my food. It passes from my mouth down a tube called the esophagus. By the time I count to eight, the food enters my stomach. Now it is on its way to being changed so my body can use it.

My stomach goes on with the job my teeth began. It squeezes and mixes and mashes the food. It breaks the food down into even smaller pieces. And it adds more juices to the food. These juices help to make the food soft.

After about two to five hours, the food moves down into my small intestine. Here, other juices, called enzymes, are added to the food. This changes the food so that my cells can use it.

Soon, the food is no longer hamburger, beans, or apple. It has been broken down, or digested, into very tiny bits called molecules. These molecules are so small they can pass through the walls of my intestine and into my blood. My blood then carries them to my cells.

Food my body can't use passes from my small intestine into another long tube called the large intestine. At the end of the large intestine is the rectum. From there, solid food waste leaves my body.

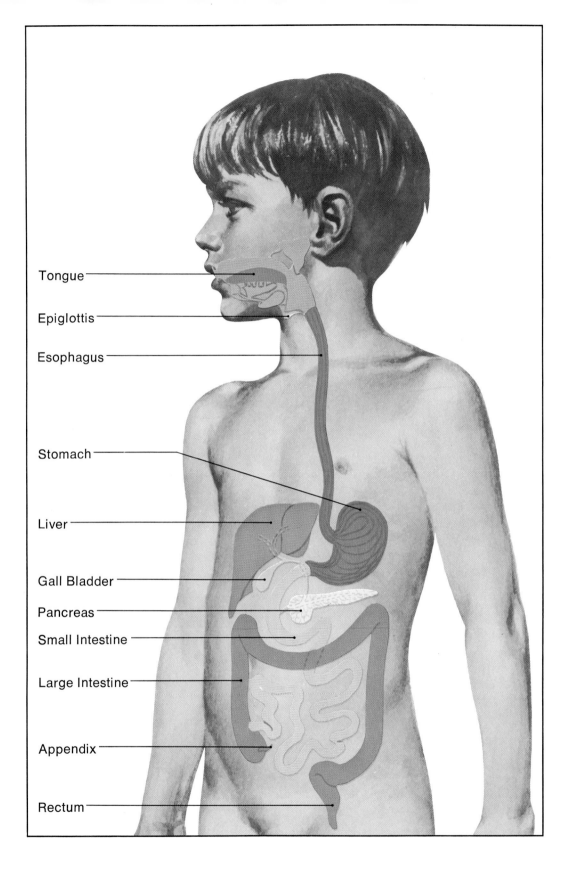

Tongue

Epiglottis

Esophagus

Stomach

Liver

Gall Bladder

Pancreas

Small Intestine

Large Intestine

Appendix

Rectum

When I am grown

I am a little girl now. But one day I will be a woman.

Now, I am kind of straight up and down. But one day my body will be more rounded.

Now, my voice is a child's voice. But one day it will be a woman's voice.

I like little babies. One day, when I am a woman, I may get married and have a baby of my own to love and care for.

I am not ready to be a mother now. My body is not ready to help make a new life begin. But the parts of me that I will need to have a baby are inside my body, growing up with me.

Two small organs, called ovaries, are inside me, near my hip bones. The ovaries make tiny eggs. Below my stomach, there is another organ called a uterus. When an egg leaves one of the ovaries, it moves down into the uterus. Then it may join with a male sperm cell to start a new life. It is here, in the uterus, that a baby grows and waits to be born.

One day, when all of me is grown up, I will be able to have a baby. I will be able to take care of a baby.

I think I will like that.

When I am grown

I am a little boy now. But one day I will be a man.

When I am grown, there will be hair on my face. If I don't want a beard, I'll have to shave every day. I'll be bigger and stronger than I am now.

When I am a man, I may want to get married and have children.

I'm not ready to be a father now. My body is not ready to help make a new life begin. But the parts of me that I will need to be a father are a part of my body right now. They are growing up with me.

Below my penis is a soft sack of skin called a scrotum. Inside my scrotum are two small organs called testicles. The testicles make sperm cells. When a sperm cell joins with a female egg, a new life may begin.

One day I'll be able to be a father. I'll love my children as much as my father and mother love me. I'll be as proud of my children as my parents are of me. I will do my best to take good care of my family.

I think I will like that.

When I bump my elbow, the nerves in my elbow send messages to my brain. I know my elbow hurts. I rub it and say, "Ouch!"

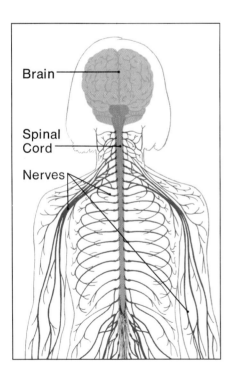

Brain

Spinal Cord

Nerves

My brain and its messengers

I can think and remember because I have a brain. I can learn to read and write because I have a brain. I can work out problems because I have a brain. And what's more, I know what my senses tell me because I have a brain.

Inside my body are thousands of nerves. These nerves are a little like tiny telephone wires. My body uses them to send messages to and from my brain.

Nerves from my eyes and ears and mouth and nose carry messages to my brain. Then my brain tells me about the messages.

If someone tickles my feet or if I bump my elbow, nerves in my body carry messages to my brain. My brain sends messages back to my feet or my elbow. Almost without thinking I do what the messages tell me to do. I giggle and I move my feet. I rub my elbow.

Messages between my brain and the rest of my body travel through my spinal cord. My spinal cord is in my spine. I can feel the bones of my spine down the center of my back.

Messages between my brain and the parts of my body move fast. They can zip up from my feet and back again more than 30 times in one second.

Inside my head

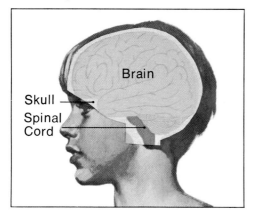

Different messages go to different parts of my brain. Sight and touch messages go to places near the surface of my brain. Smell, taste, and hearing messages go deeper into my brain.

Different parts of my brain get different messages

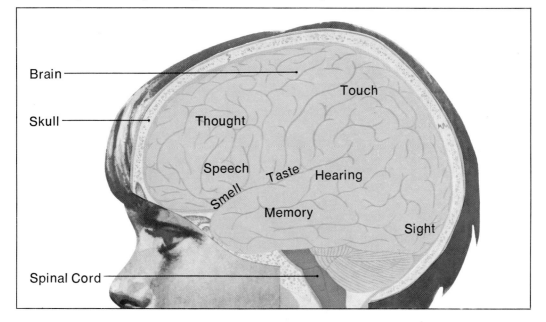

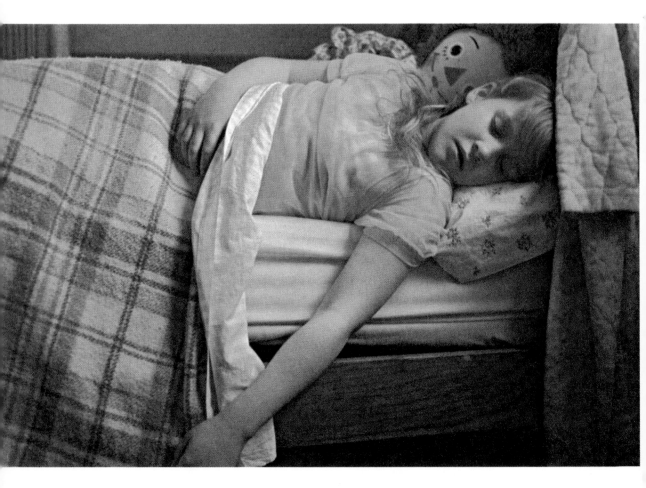

My brain takes care of me

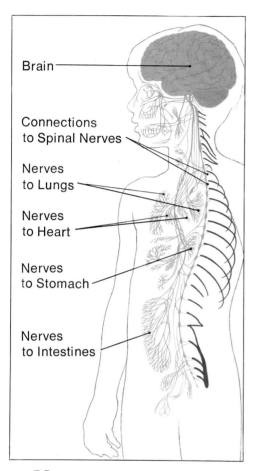

Brain

Connections
to Spinal Nerves

Nerves
to Lungs

Nerves
to Heart

Nerves
to Stomach

Nerves
to Intestines

My nerves carry messages from my brain to my heart, my stomach, and to other organs in my body. The messages keep these organs working. I don't have to think about them.

My brain is busy taking care of me even when I don't think about it. My lungs breathe in fresh air and breathe out used air. My heart pumps blood through my body. My stomach and intestines digest my food even while I'm sleeping. My brain is always sending messages through my nerves to make these things happen.

When my body needs to get rid of wastes, nerves in my bladder and rectum send messages to my brain. My brain tells me about the messages.

Sometimes when I'm sick I throw up. My brain tells the muscles in my chest and stomach what to do, and the food in my stomach rushes back up my esophagus and out my mouth. My mouth tastes sour after I throw up because of the stomach juices mixed with the food.

My brain tells me when I'm sleepy. When I'm asleep, it sends messages to my muscles to keep me from rolling off my bed. When I've slept long enough, my brain awakens me.

I'm glad I don't have to think about getting so many jobs done. If I did I'd never have time for fun!

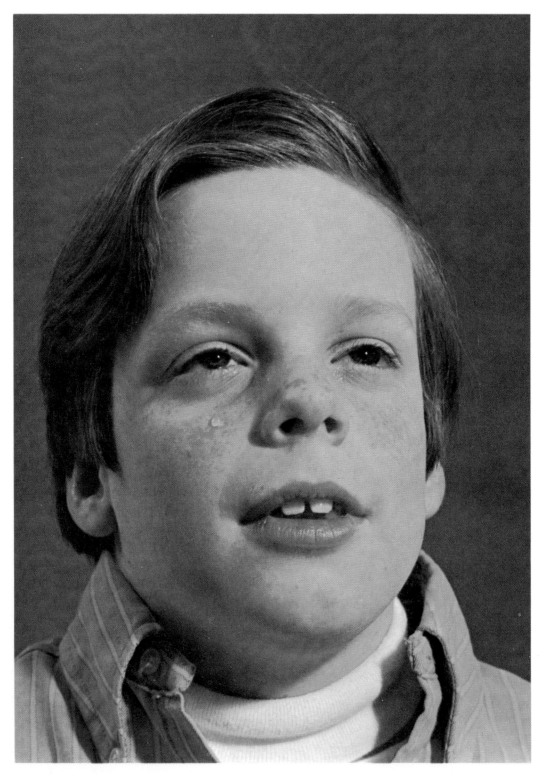

Outside my eye

Ouch! Something's in my eye! I'm not crying, but my eye is. It's crying tears just as if I really were sad. That happens whenever specks of dust and dirt get past my eyelashes and into one of my eyes. Tears wash away the specks.

In fact, I always have tears in my eyes. That's why my eyes look shiny. The tears come from little holes behind my eyelids. When I blink, my eyelids spread the tears across my eyes. The tears clean my eyes and keep them wet. If I try not to blink, my eyes start to sting. That's because they're drying off and need more tears.

If I could look behind my eyelids I'd see that my eyes are almost as round as balls. That's why they're called eyeballs.

My eyeballs are in my skull. They are protected by bones and layers of fat around them. If something hits my face, the bones are hit first and my eyeballs are not usually harmed.

Inside my eye

My eyes and my brain work together. Here's how.

When I look at a thing, the light that bounces off of it enters my eye through a clear covering called the cornea. The light touches nerves at the back of the eye. The nerves send messages about the light to my brain. When my brain gets the messages, I know I'm seeing something.

The colored circle in my eye is the iris. In the center of the iris is a dark spot called the pupil. The pupil is the hole that lets light into my eye.

Muscles in the iris make the pupil bigger or smaller to let in more or less light. The darker a place, the larger my pupil gets. The brighter a place, the smaller my pupil gets.

Behind the pupil is the lens. The lens is clear. Light passes through it.

The inside of my eye is filled with clear liquid that is a little like jelly. Light passes through that, too. The light touches the back of my eye where the tiny nerves are.

These nerves send their messages to a big nerve. The messages travel along the big nerve to my brain. My brain understands them. I see. And I know that I see.

I see my eye

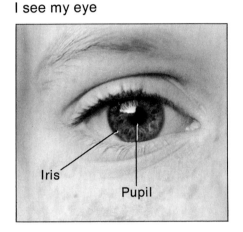

Iris

Pupil

One of my eyes

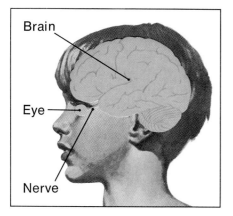

There are more than a hundred thousand nerves in my retina. Light touches the nerves, and the nerves send messages about the light to my brain.

Inside my eyeball

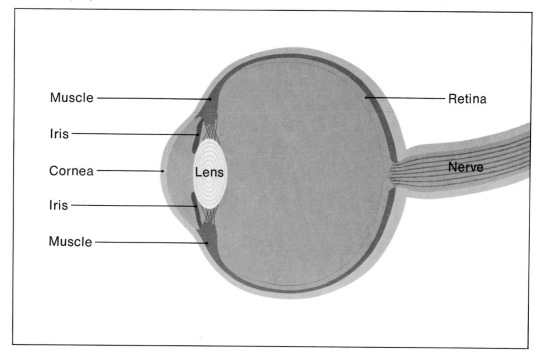

Sometimes eyes need help

I see a horse in a field. If I can't see the horse clearly, my eyes need help.

Eyeballs should be nearly round. People whose eyeballs are too long are nearsighted. They look at the far-off horse, and they see only a blur. A clear picture of the horse does not form at the back of their eyes. Nearsighted people wear glasses to help them see things that are far away.

People whose eyeballs are too short are farsighted. When they look at something close by, such as the words in this book, they see a blur. Farsighted people wear glasses to help them see things that are nearby.

Some people wear contact lenses instead of glasses. Contact lenses are made of clear plastic. They are so small that they float on the tears that cover the eyes. The fronts of the eyes over the irises are rounded. Contact lenses are also rounded. The lenses fit over the irises and stay in place until the people who wear the contact lenses take them out of their eyes.

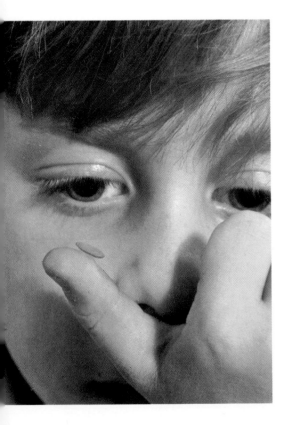

My sister's contact lenses are smaller than the tip of my thumb.

If my eyeballs were too long, I'd be nearsighted. Then, a far-off horse might look like this to me. My eyes would need help.

I'd wear the kind of glasses that helped my eyes see far-off things clearly. Then, the horse that was far off would look like this to me.

My ears

People talk to me. Car horns honk. Dogs bark. Music is somewhere nearby. I know about these sounds because my ears and my brain work together.

My ears turn sounds into nerve messages. Nerves in my ears carry the messages to my brain. And my brain understands them. This is how that happens.

Sounds are air waves. The air waves enter my ear and bump against my eardrum. My eardrum moves when airwaves hit it.

When my eardrum moves, it bumps into three small bones called the hammer, the anvil, and the stirrup. As these bones bump against each other, the stirrup moves in and out of an opening in a place that looks like a snail shell. This place is called the cochlea. Inside the cochlea are liquid and nerves. As the stirrup moves in and out of the opening of the cochlea, it makes waves in the liquid. The waves move across the nerves.

When that happens, the nerves carry messages to my brain. My brain tells me there's a sound. And it tells me what kind of sound I hear.

So, if somebody speaks to me, I know it. If a horn honks, I know it. And if a dog barks, I know that, too. I hear!

The parts of my ear

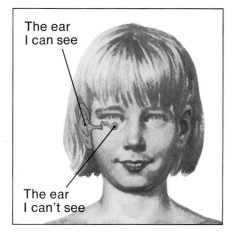

The ear
I can see

The ear
I can't see

I can touch only part of my ear. Most of my ear is inside my head. Some parts of my ear don't show on this picture. These parts help me to keep my balance. You can read about them on pages 84 and 85.

Parts that help me hear

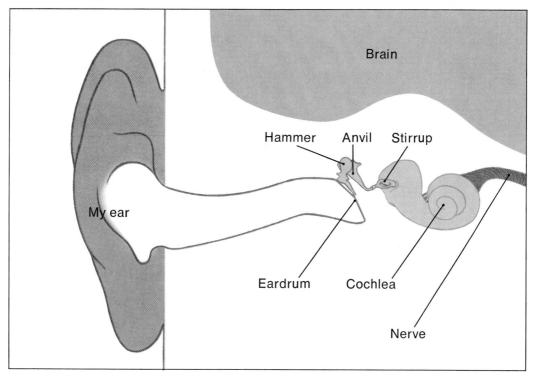

Brain

Hammer   Anvil   Stirrup

My ear

Eardrum   Cochlea

Nerve

Sometimes ears need help

In quiet rooms I can hear the softest sounds—the tick-tock of the clock, my baby sister's breathing while she sleeps.

In noisy places I have to listen harder to hear what people say. Sometimes I put my hand to my ear and make kind of a cup to catch the sounds so they will go into the tunnel of my ear. My ears are fine, yet sometimes I use my hand to help my ears.

My friend Johnny does not hear as well as I do. His ears need help all the time. He wears a hearing aid. I can see a button in his ear and a wire that goes from the button to a small box he carries with him. The box catches sounds and makes them louder. The sounds go through the wire to the button and then into the tunnel of Johnny's ear.

Some people wear hearing aids that I can't see at first. My cousin wears "hearing glasses" that have a hearing aid hidden in the frames. Some hearing aids are so small they fit right into the ear and have no wires or boxes that I can see.

But all hearing aids are a little like tiny telephones because they catch sounds and carry them right to the ear.

Hearing aids help these children
to hear the voice of the police
officer.

Keeping my balance

My inner ear does more than help me hear. It has another big job—it helps me keep my balance.

It helps me stay upright when I am moving. And it helps me stay upright when I am standing still.

Inside my inner ear are three small hollow loops filled with liquid. These are my balance tubes. At the bottom of each loop are tiny cells that look like hairs. Leading from each hair-cell is a nerve.

When I move my head, the liquid in the loops moves across the hair-cells. The nerves send messages to my brain. Then my brain sends messages to the muscles in my body. These messages help me keep my balance when I walk or run or skip or hop or jump.

The parts of my ear

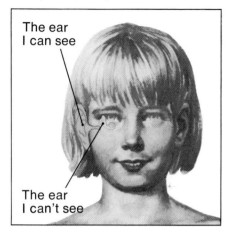

The ear
I can see

The ear
I can't see

The balance tubes are a part of my ear that is inside my head. Other parts of my inner ear help me to hear. You can read about these other parts on pages 80 and 81.

Parts that help me keep my balance

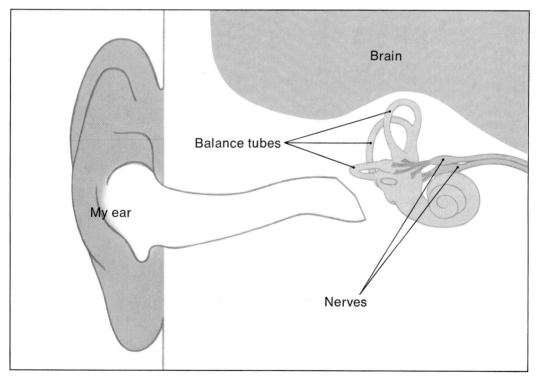

Brain

Balance tubes

My ear

Nerves

My nose

I can see part of my nose, the part that sticks out from my face. The holes in my nose are called nostrils. Hairs grow in my nostrils. The hairs help keep dust out of my nose.

But I can't see all of my nose. Behind the part I see is a large tunnel. This tunnel is called the nasal cavity. The walls of the tunnel are wet and warm. They are covered with a sticky liquid. This liquid is called mucus. Mucus helps trap dust or germs that get past the hairs in my nostrils. When I sneeze or blow my nose, I get rid of the dust and germs.

Millions of dust specks enter my nose every time I breathe. Most of these are caught by the hairs in my nostrils and the mucus in my nasal cavity. If they weren't caught, I would slowly get a lot of dust in my lungs.

My nose warms the air I breathe. My nose helps to clean the air I breathe. And my nose helps me to smell.

The nose I can't see

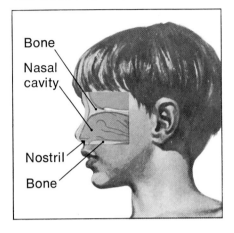

My nasal cavity

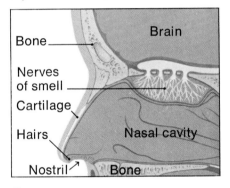

Inside my nasal cavity are nerves that pick up messages and send them to my brain. My brain receives these messages and tells me what I am smelling.

How I smell food

I smell chocolate cake. The smell is really tiny bits that have broken away from the cake and float in the air. The bits are called molecules. The molecules are too small to see. But they can't fool my nose.

Inside my nose are many hairlike nerves. When a smell enters my nostrils, the nerves send the message to my brain. My brain tells me what I smell.

My sense of smell also helps my body get ready to digest my food. When I smell something good to eat, my brain sends messages to the glands that make my saliva and stomach juices. My mouth waters and my stomach glands start making their juices before I even chew my first bite.

How I taste food

Yum! There's ice cream for dessert! Ugh! I have to eat my beets first.

I know what I like and what I don't like because I can taste my food. My tongue rolls each bite around my mouth. I taste my food as it tumbles over my tongue.

The front, back, and edges of my tongue are covered with little bumps. On the sides of the bumps are tiny openings to my taste buds. Inside the taste buds are nerves that send messages to my brain. My brain tells me what I'm tasting.

The nerves in my lips, tongue, teeth, and mouth, and my jaw muscles also help me know what I'm eating. They send messages to my brain about how hot or cold my food is, and whether it's rough or smooth, hard or soft.

My food tastes better when I can smell it. When a cold stops up my nose, food doesn't taste as good. And food tastes better when I can see it, too.

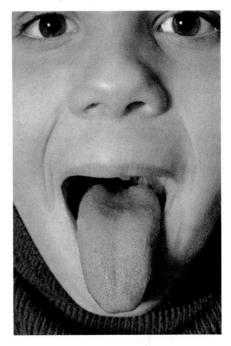

I see my tongue

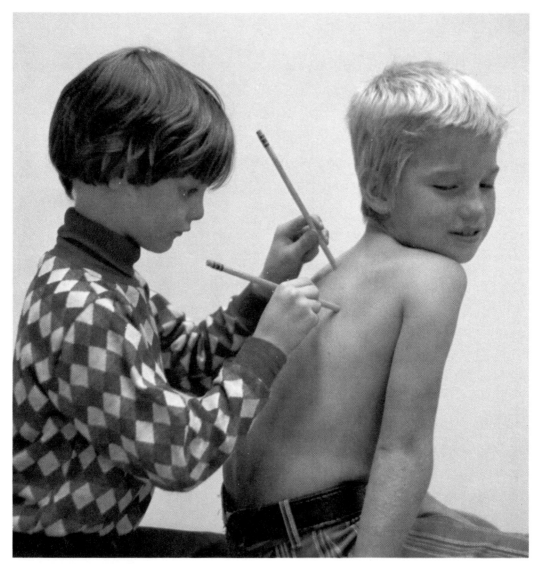

The nerves in my back are farther apart than the nerves in my fingers. My friend touches my back with two unsharpened pencils. Both pencils touch my back at the same time. But I can feel only one until the two pencils are quite far apart.

My sense of touch

A pin feels sharp. An apple feels smooth. Ice feels cold. A pillow feels soft. I know what all these things feel like because of nerves in my skin.

The nerves in my fingers are very close together. That's why my fingers are good feelers. Suppose I ring a bicycle bell on a hot day. Some of my nerves tell me that the bell is very hot. Other nerves tell me that it is smooth. Still other nerves tell me how hard I'm pushing. And perhaps some of my nerves tell me that my finger is sore.

I see only with my eyes. I hear only with my ears. I smell only with my nose. I taste only with my mouth. But I feel things all over my body.

My body does wonderful things

All the parts of me work together, helping each other.

My lungs take air into my body. My brain, muscles, and bones help my lungs.

In order to move, my bones need help. My muscles help my bones move.

My brain thinks and sends messages to all the parts of me. My brain needs oxygen. It gets oxygen from my blood.

My bones, muscles, brain, lungs, heart, nerves, and stomach all help each other. I take care of my body so it can do all these things.

I keep clean. I brush my teeth. I take baths. I wash my hands before I eat.

I eat the kinds of food my body needs to grow, to keep warm, to work properly.

I get plenty of sleep.

I get lots of fresh air. I run and jump and climb and play games. This helps my muscles grow strong.

I'm careful about touching sharp things. I'm careful about where I swim. I'm careful about crossing streets.

I'm human, and I'm made of human parts. I don't have a bear's hair or a hen's skin or a gull's skull or a fly's eyes or a steer's ears. I'm me, and all my parts work together to make me what I am. Taking care of me—that's my job!

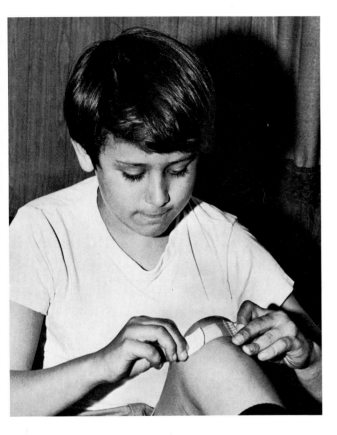

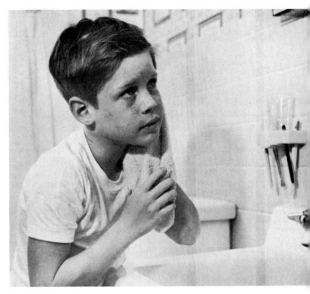

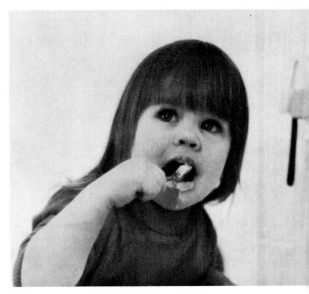

Becoming Me

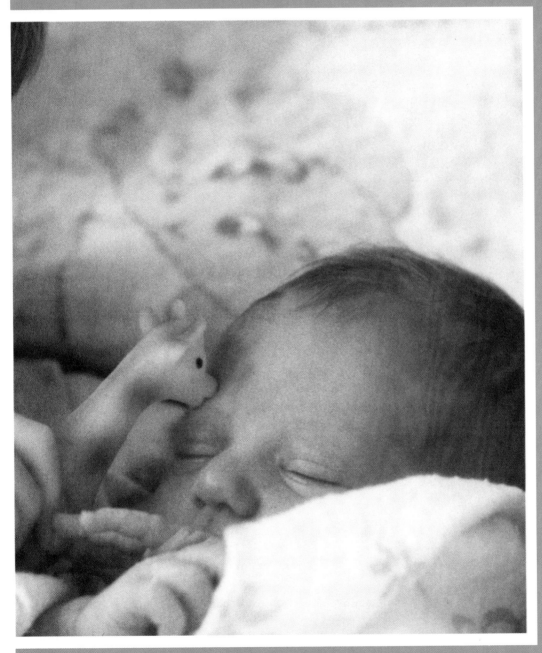

Before I was born

Where was I before I was born? I was warm and safe inside my mother's body, in a special place beneath her stomach. I was there because my mother and my father loved each other and wanted me. This is how it happened.

Inside of my mother was a special kind of cell—an egg. It was smaller than a grain of salt, smaller than the tiny dot I make with my pencil.

Inside of my father was another special cell called a sperm. It was smaller even than the egg, smaller than the tiniest speck of dust.

The sperm cell and the egg cell came together inside my mother's body. They became one cell. When that happened, a new life began, my life. I began to be the child I am now.

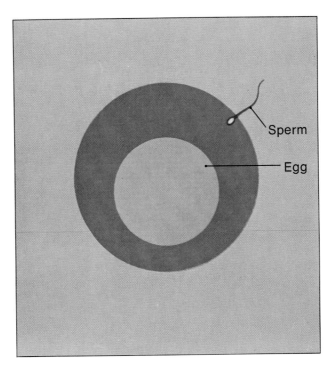

An egg is smaller than a tiny dot.
A sperm is even tinier. But when
an egg and a sperm come together,
a new life begins.

Waiting to be born

I had a lot of growing to do before I would be ready to be born. The egg and the sperm which had joined to make my life found a waiting place in which to grow. The waiting place was the uterus in my mother's body. I was safe and warm there, and I was fed through a cord that joined me to my mother.

Soon the cell that was to become me began to divide. It divided into two cells. The two cells divided into four. The four cells divided into eight. The eight cells divided into sixteen cells. The tiny jelly-like cells stayed close together, and the dividing went on and on.

At first all of the cells seemed to be alike. But after a while each cell began to do a special job. Some cells became skin cells. Others became bone cells, heart cells, brain cells.

That is the way I grew before I was born. I grew and changed shape and grew and changed shape. As I grew, my mother's uterus became larger to make room for me.

I began to move about. I waved my arms. I kicked my legs. My mother could feel me moving and growing larger, and she and my father were very happy.

For nine months I grew and changed shape.

One cell

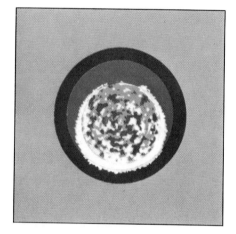

The cell divided

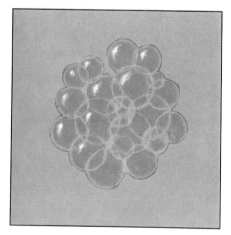

The egg cell and the sperm became one cell. Soon the cell divided. It became two cells. The dividing went on. At the end of a week there were many cells, all together in a little ball.

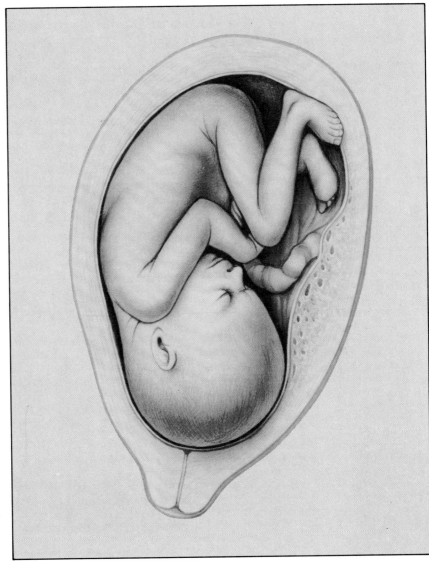

After about four and a half months, the ball of cells had changed into a perfect baby. The baby grew in its mother's body until it was time to be born.

I am born

Early one morning my mother felt a pushing inside her. The pushing stopped, then it started. It stopped and started, stopped and started again. Each time the pushing became stronger.

My mother knew what the pushing meant. It was a signal that I was ready to be born. The muscles of her uterus were pushing me out into the world.

My father took my mother to the hospital. She was not sick, but she and I needed help. The doctors and nurses would help us.

In the hospital, a nurse took my mother to a special room where babies are born. The muscles of her uterus were pushing harder and harder. My mother waited. At last my head pushed out of her body, through her vagina. Slowly, slowly, the rest of me came out, too.

My mother heard me cry. She smiled. Then the doctor cut the cord that joined me to her. I no longer needed it.

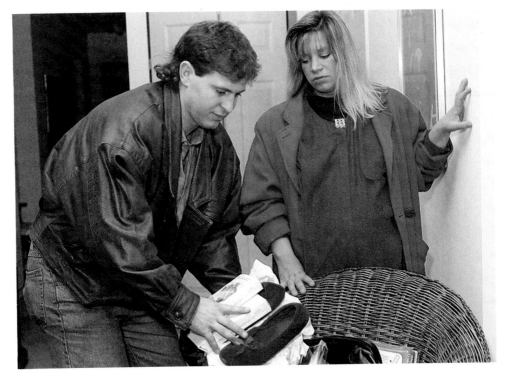

When it was time to go to the hospital,
Father helped Mother get ready.

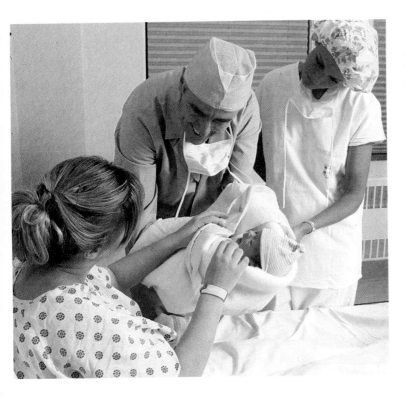

I left Mother's body. The
doctor helped me breathe.
He held me up so Mother
could see me.

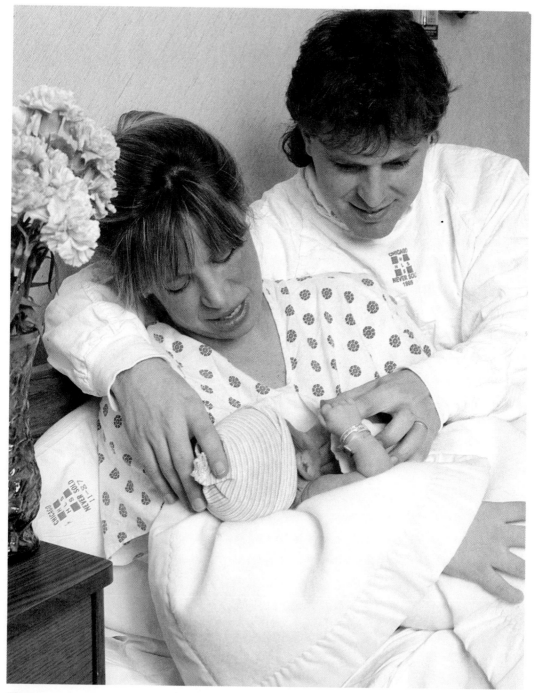

Father came to Mother's hospital
room to see us. I held his finger
in my hand.

In the hospital

Now my mother rested. And the doctor and nurse did many things for me.

They put drops in my eyes to keep them healthy. They looked at my ears and nose, and fingers and toes—all of me.

Name tags were put around my wrist and ankle. A nurse put ink on my fingers and feet and made fingerprints and foot-prints on paper. They were different from those of every other baby in the world. The nurse put the paper into a folder with my name on it.

The nurse weighed me and measured me. I got a bath and was dressed in a shirt and diaper and nightgown. Next I was wrapped in a warm blanket and given a drink of water. Then I was tucked into a small bed in a room with lots of other babies.

I was all tired out. I just closed my eyes and went to sleep.

After a while I woke up. I cried. The nurse carried me to my mother. My mother smiled at me and held me close.

I wore a name tag on my wrist and my ankle. Now, everyone knew who I was.

In my new home

After a few days in the hospital my mother and I were ready to go home. The nurse dressed me, wrapped me in a blanket, and handed me to my mother.

My father came. He looked at the bracelet on my wrist. "This baby's ours," he said. He hugged my mother and me. And then all of us went home, my father, my mother, and me.

I had many things to do in my new house. At first I just cried and ate and slept. I ate both day and night. I yawned. I slept, and I slept some more.

After a while I stayed awake longer each day. I learned to like my bath. I even learned to splash in the water. I liked to stretch and stretch.

I grew. And I learned some more things. I learned to know my parents' voices. I learned to know my name. I turned my head when they called me.

My mother said, "How fast our baby is growing!"

I kept on growing and learning. I gurgled when my mother fed me. I learned to play with my fingers and to shake my rattle. After a while I could even sit up. Then I could see all around me.

"Our baby is growing up," my father said.

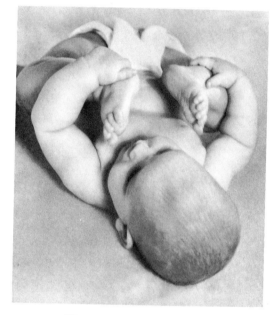

Each day I found something new to play with—first my fingers, then my toes.

I learned to like my bath. I liked the feeling of warm water on my back.

I get to know my big sister. She is already one of my favorite people.

Whom will I look like?

I have been growing ever since that time. Sometimes I wonder whom I will look like when I grow up. Will I look like my father? Will I be as tall as he is? Will I look like my mother? Will I have pretty hands like hers?

I will look a little like both my father and my mother. And I will look a little like my grandparents and my great-grandparents as well.

Something was passed along to me from both of my parents in the egg cell and the sperm cell that joined to become me. In the egg cell in my mother were tiny things

called genes. In the sperm cell that came from my father there were more genes.

Each of the genes was like an order. One of the genes was an order for height. Another was an order for hair color. Still another was an order for eye color. There were thousands of such orders. All together these orders were like a building plan. All together they told my body how to grow into the special person that is me.

Whom will I look like when I grow up? I will look a little like my father . . . a little like my mother . . . a little like my grand-parents. Mostly, I will look like ME.

Brothers and sisters are a little alike because they have genes from the same parents. But their genes aren't exactly alike. Identical twins look alike because their genes are alike or nearly alike.

Dad looks like his parents.
Sister and Brother look like Dad,
Mother, Grandma, and Grandpa.

Me and My Family

My family

Maybe I live with my natural parents, the mother and father to whom I was born. We love each other. We are a family.

But maybe I do not live with my natural parents.

Maybe I was adopted. My mother and father chose me to be part of their family. I love them and they love me. And we are a family.

Jerry and Marty are adopted. David and Phil are not. They all live together and love each other. They are a family.

Maybe I live with my mother and my stepfather. Or maybe I live with my father and my stepmother. They take care of me. We love each other. And we

are a family.

Maybe I live alone with my mother. We love each other. We are a family.

Or maybe I live alone with my father. We love each other. We are a family, too.

There are many kinds of families. Each person thinks his kind is the very best.

Here's what we do for each other in our family. Most families do the same.

We stick up for each other.

We are glad and sad with each other.

We work and play together.

We share things.

Most of all, we love each other.

We are a family!

George lives with his mother. They love and need each other. They are a family. They like to work and play together.

Nancy lives with her father. The two of them are a family. They love and need each other. They like being together.

Sometimes when I tell my Dad
that I don't want to go to bed,
he tells me that I have to.

Do I have to?

My puppy stays up as late as he likes.
I have to go to bed early.

My puppy doesn't have to go to school. And we always put away his toys.

I have to pick up my own toys. And I have to go to school every day.

Sometimes I wish I were a puppy!

If I were a puppy I would stay up as late as I liked and go to bed whenever I pleased. And I would play outdoors all day long and never go to school.

Then I remember that puppies at our house can't do everything they want to.

Puppies must not chew slippers, even when they want to.

Puppies must not bring bones into the living room, even when they want to.

Puppies must not jump onto beds, even when they want to. And puppies at our house have to eat in the kitchen.

My puppy "has to." I "have to." And what's more, so do lots of people.

Mom and Dad "have to" work, even when they don't want to. And they "have to" work at the same time every day.

Grandmother has to take medicine every day. I know she doesn't like it, because she makes a funny face.

Everybody "has to," I guess.

"Do I have to?" Yes!

All those people

Some children have many brothers and sisters.

Some children have only one or two brothers or sisters.

And some children have no brothers or sisters at all.

But all children have grandparents. I have two grandmas and two grandpas.

One of my grandmas is my father's mother, and one of my grandmas is my mother's mother.

One of my grandpas is my mother's father, and one of my grandpas is my father's father.

I have aunts and uncles, also.

Some of my aunts are my mother's sisters, and some are my father's sisters.

Some of my uncles are my father's brothers, and some of my uncles are my mother's brothers.

My aunts and uncles have husbands and wives, and they are my uncles and aunts, too.

Most of my aunts and uncles have children. The children are my cousins.

My parents have many brothers and sisters, so I have many uncles and aunts and cousins. There are many families. We are related to each other. Together, we form one big family group.

My family tree

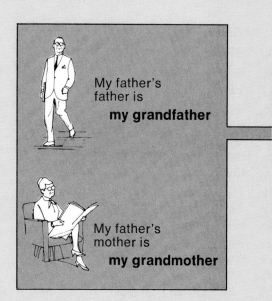

My father's father is **my grandfather**

My father's mother is **my grandmother**

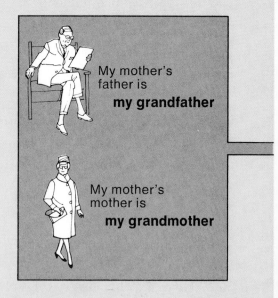

My mother's father is **my grandfather**

My mother's mother is **my grandmother**

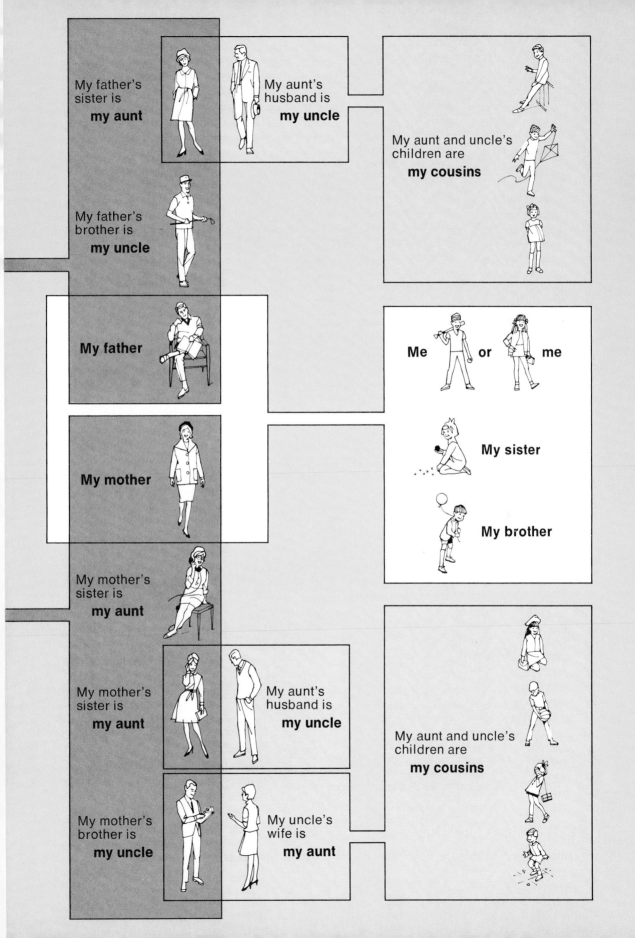

My father's sister is **my aunt**

My aunt's husband is **my uncle**

My aunt and uncle's children are **my cousins**

My father's brother is **my uncle**

My father

Me or me

My mother

My sister

My brother

My mother's sister is **my aunt**

My mother's sister is **my aunt**

My aunt's husband is **my uncle**

My aunt and uncle's children are **my cousins**

My mother's brother is **my uncle**

My uncle's wife is **my aunt**

Families everywhere

I know that my family does some things differently from the ways other families in the world do the same things. But I also know that families—no matter where they live—do some things in the same way. This is especially true of the children in the family.

Children learn to do many things from their fathers. (Ivory Coast)

Older children look after younger children in the family. (Turkey)

Children like to spend time with their grandmothers. (Czechoslovakia)

They visit their uncles, aunts, and cousins. (West Germany)

Sometimes, they listen to the radio with the whole family. (Niger)

They take walks with their parents. (Japan)

In families everywhere, people take care of each other and share happy times together.

Working together

In my family, we all help when certain jobs need to be done. When we work together, things get done more quickly and more easily. And lots of times it's more fun. Children in families all over the world help out in the same way.

Children help carry coconuts to market. (Fiji Islands)

Children help in the kitchen. (United States)

Everybody works together at harvest times. (West Germany)

Everybody helps carry home a crop of hay. (Italy)

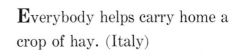

And everybody helps sell things. (Mexico)

In families everywhere, people help each other by working together.

Children play in the snow. (Arctic)

Children play

I play with my family and my friends. I like to play guessing games and spelling games. I also like to shout, run, jump, climb, dance, skate, and play hide-and-seek.

When I play, I exercise my mind and my body.

Children roller-skate. (France)

Children play games during recess. (China)

Children play team games such as soccer. (Denmark)

Playing is an important part of growing up for children everywhere.

People pray

Throughout the world, people show their belief in a power that is greater than man. Some people show their faith by praying together or alone. Others hold celebrations.

Children celebrate a Shinto religious holiday. (Japan)

A family gives thanks to God for
what it has received. (United States)

Children learn things

Before I went to school, my parents taught me much about my world. Now I also learn in school. I study my lessons. I practice. I need to know and do many things so that when I grow up I will be ready to take my place in the world.

Children everywhere learn to keep their bodies healthy. (India)

Children everywhere practice their music lessons. (Taiwan)

Children everywhere learn how to study. (Panama Canal Zone)

For children everywhere, learning is important.

Happy times together

Families often take pictures of some of the happy things they do together during vacation times. Then, later on, they can look at the pictures and have almost as much fun just remembering and talking about the good times they shared.

Families everywhere share happy times in a favorite spot. (France)

Families everywhere enjoy visiting unusual places. (Italy)

Families everywhere go for outings in the park. (England)

No matter where they live, people enjoy the vacations they spend with the family.

My Widening World

My door opens

At first my world was small. It was only as big as my mother's arms. Then my bed and my room became part of my world. One day my mother carried me to the window. I reached for the sunshine on the window. My world grew bigger. Soon my home and the things in it were part of my world. As I grew, my world grew. But my home is still the place where my day begins and ends.

I know my house so well I can find things in the dark. My sense of touch tells me, "Brick is rough, tile is smooth, and the cactus in the pot is prickly." I

At first my world was small.

It widened as I learned to crawl.

know where the cat sleeps. We have a bell that makes a lovely sound when I shake it. We even have places filled with odds and ends that make our home different from any other home.

When I am in my home I am in a special world that I share with my family. My parents have filled our home with toys, books, pictures, a radio, a television set, a stove, a refrigerator, and many other things for us to use and enjoy.

Our home is a private place. But when friends knock on the door, we say, "Come in." We have extra chairs for friends. A home that is ready for friends opens the door to a wider world.

Then I walked. I could explore . . .

The big world beyond my door.

My house is like your house

I wondered about the big house on my block. One day my mother and I went there to visit. I saw tables, chairs, beds, and cupboards. I told the owner, "Your house is like my house."

I visited a small house. I saw windows, doors, ceilings, walls, and floors. I said, "My house is like your house."

One house was big. The other was small. Yet they were alike because both houses were built for people to live in.

Not all people need the same kind of house. My grandparents once lived in a big house. Then their children grew up and had houses of their own. My grandparents live in a small apartment now. It is just right for them.

My uncle moves his trailer-house when he goes to a new job. A house that can be moved from place to place is right for him.

My cousin lives in a townhouse.

A house may be made of brick, wood, cement, or even blocks of ice. It may be big, small, plain, or beautiful. My house is a safe place. It is the place where I eat, sleep, and rest. It is the place I know and love. When I am rested I am eager to leave my house to explore new places. But I always come home.

The house I live in is built of brick and stone. It's the place I call home.

My uncle lives in a trailer.
It is very different from my
house. It is my uncle's home.

Grandma and Grandpa live in a
small apartment in a big building.
It is their home.

My world stretches out

When I leave my house, my world stretches out around me. People are in my world. I like to know what they are doing, so I walk around my block.

I smell cookies baking.

I hear boys and girls yelling.

I watch people cutting lawns, painting fences, and washing cars. I watch the garbage truck stop at every house.

Sometimes I scratch a puppy behind the ears. Or I watch a cat climb a tree.

I smell hot tar and run to watch men mend my street. Car horns honk.

I speak to the mail carrier, to Mrs. Jones next door, and to children on their way to school.

I watch a crossing guard stop the cars so children can cross the street safely.

When I reach the end of my block, another block stretches ahead. On my left and on my right are still other blocks.

Those blocks are filled with houses. The houses are homes for people. I wonder how many people and how many blocks are in my city. How much space on the earth does my block fill?

My eyes tell me those other blocks must be much like mine. But I know mine is a very special block. I live here.

I leave my block

I used to ride in a grocery cart when we shopped for food. Now my folks send me to the store for things they forgot to buy. Today I have to buy oatmeal.

I walk down the aisles in the store. I must pay attention if I am to find the oatmeal among the cans, boxes, bottles, and bags that fill the shelves. I get hungry when I see all that food. But I like to look at it. The oranges, apples, cabbages, and tomatoes in the trays are as bright as the new crayons in my box. I see people choose food, and I think, "A store is a big cupboard for a neighborhood."

As I walk through the store, I watch the people who work there. I see them putting boxes and cans on shelves. I see someone weighing onions on a scale. Another person is counting ears of corn.

I find the box of oatmeal and take it to the place where I can pay for it. The cashier looks at it and punches numbers on a machine. The machine shows how much I must pay. The cashier takes my money and counts my change. I think, "A store is a big arithmetic problem. It must be hard to know what so many numbers mean."

I left my house and my block to run an errand. I've done it once. I know that I can do it again.

The first time I went to school, my
mother walked with me.

At school, I learned many things,
including the names of colors.

The first day

Going to school on the first day of the new school year is always exciting. I wake up early in the morning. I'm too excited to eat much of my breakfast. I don't want to be late for school.

What will my new teacher be like?

What will my new room be like?

Where will I sit?

What new books will I have? They will be more grown-up than last year's books.

I haven't seen some of my friends all summer. There will be lots to talk about. And there will be new boys and girls in my room, new friends for me.

It will all be strange at first. But I know that soon everything will be friendly and familiar. Soon we'll study and do things together.

The first time I went to school I was afraid. I didn't know how things would be. I was shy with so many children all around me. Then I wanted to lead in every way. But everyone can't be first. We all learned to take turns. I learned new things. I got used to it all.

Long roads

I like to travel with my family. I go to the gas station with my mother. The garage man checks our car for safety.

We go back home and I sit on top of a big suitcase so Dad can close it. And then we're ready.

While I ride I look at road maps. My state looks small on a map, but, oh, there are long roads between cities. I see the bridges, tunnels, lakes, rivers, farms, factories, and forests, and I know my state is not small, but big.

When we travel, I never know what I will see next. A pet monkey with clothes on. A marching band. A truckload of cows. And people, people, people.

Sometimes we sleep in a motel. Sometimes we sleep in a friend's house. Each morning before we leave I must be sure we have not forgotten anything.

I like to go away. But when we are almost home, I wonder how my house will look and if my friends will welcome me. I always find that my house looks fine. My friends shout, "Come play!"

I like to travel with my family. Sometimes we stop at a motel to sleep. It's fun to stop at a different place every day.

The motel has a swimming pool. I like that. I'm glad when Dad says, "How about going for a swim?"

I like to eat in the motel restaurant. I can choose what I want from a long list of good things.

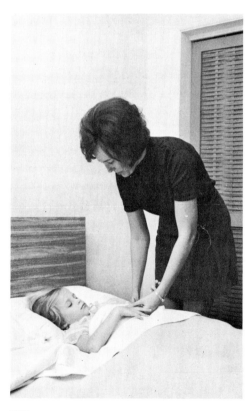

When it's time to go to bed, Mother tucks me in. I'm tired. I fall asleep as soon as my head touches the pillow.

Morning comes. I want to be on our way. Mother and Dad show us a line on the map. They say, "We'll take this road today."

Friends share my widening world

I am growing up. To grow is to learn. I like the people who help me grow. I learn many things from friends my own age and from my family, my doctor, my dentist, my teachers, and lots of other grown-ups. They are all my friends.

My uncle is my friend. He lets me help when he works on his car. I watch him when he changes the oil and checks the battery.

The grown-ups I know are busy people. I like to watch while the garbage collector works. I talk to the clerks who sell food, clothes, and toys. I talk to the librarian, to

the people who cut the grass in the park, to the lifeguard at the pool. They always say "hello" when they see me.

The police officer on the corner is my friend. The officer helps me cross the street when I go to school or when I come home from school.

My grandfather is my friend, too. He knows how to do lots of things. When my bicycle was broken, he showed me how to fix it.

I feel friendly toward all these people and lots of others. I want and need friends to share my widening world.

Getting ready

I said to my father and my mother, "Someday I will grow up. I will leave home. When that day comes, will I be ready?"

"Yes," said my father. "You were getting ready to leave home when you took your first step. Getting to know your family, your house, your block, your school, and your town are all part of getting ready to leave home."

My mother said, "Your growing-up years are filled with things for you to explore. You will keep forever the things that you learn. They will be there for you to use when you need them. You will be ready."

I like to explore new places. I also like to go back to favorite places and to the people I like. When I go back, my five senses help me remember the places and the people I have known. I always learn something new.

If I have children of my own, I will take them to my old house. I will show them around. I will say, "This is where the floor used to squeak. And right here is where my cat used to sleep."

I will hear my children say, "Grandpa, Grandma." My senses will help me explore this home I once knew.

I dream of far places

Up in the sky, jet planes leave vapor trails. They look like white zippers in blue cloth. I think, "Who is up there? Where are they going? What will they see?" I whisper strange names of places—Honolulu, Walla Walla, Singapore, and Oslo. I read place names on a map. The words change into a singing kind of poetry. I think, "Who lives there? What are their houses like? What do they eat?"

Some of my toys were made in Japan.

The coffee we use grew in Brazil.

My brother's sweater was made in Scotland.

We have a typewriter from Italy.

I watch news programs on television. I hear people in faraway places speak Chinese, Spanish, or German. I see the shapes of mountains and elephants. I see a clock in London called Big Ben.

I am not old enough to know much about the world—but, oh! I am old enough to be curious. Someday I will go north, south, east, and west. I will explore new sights, sounds, smells, and tastes. But I will come home again.

Life on earth changes

I am young. But the world is old. Each day it changes. It becomes more crowded with people and things. By the time I have grown up, many things will change. Some things will even disappear. New things will take their place.

Before I grow old, I may not live above the ground, but deep inside a mountain. There I will push buttons to get the air, light, and heat I must have to live. I may take a trip to the moon. I may live on a satellite far out in space. Maybe I'll live in a great plastic bubble at the bottom of the sea. Much of the food I eat may come from special farms in the sea. Gold and copper may come from mines in the sea instead of from mines on land.

My children may go to a school that is different from the one I now go to. Perhaps they will not go to a school at all. Instead they may study their lessons from a big television screen on a wall in our house. I may sit at a television desk and read any book I choose from any library in the world.

The world and the people and things in it will change. But things that seem strange to me today will no longer be that way. My five senses will always help me fit into the world around me.

I see

I touch

My senses guide me

The circle of my world grows wider every day. But I always remain at the center of my world. Each time I move, my circle moves. I can move across, down into, or above the ground. Astronauts move away from the earth. Someday even I may fly into outer space.

As long as I live, move, and use my five senses, my world will keep growing.

My five senses guard my body. They warn me of danger. They help me learn about the things in my world.

My mind stores the things that my senses help me learn. I remember when something is dangerous. And I remember things that made me happy or sad.

I know that a lemon is sour and that sugar is sweet because I have tasted them. Once I picked a rose. A sharp point on its stem stuck into my finger. It hurt. I was careful the next time I picked a rose.

I have five senses and a mind. They protect me and help me know my world. If I learn to use them well, my world will grow ever wider.

I hear

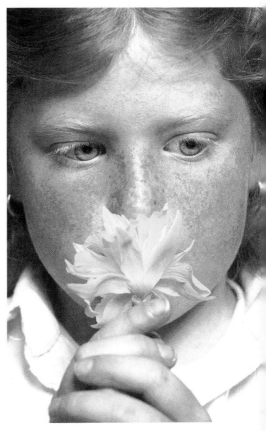

I smell

I taste

Watch Me Grow

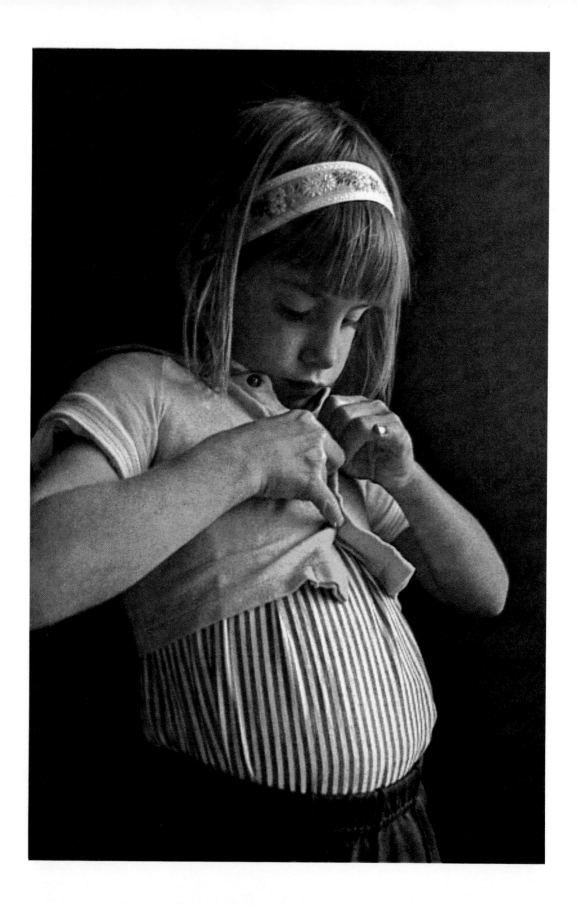

I grow

I am always growing. Growing is the easiest thing I do. I don't have to think about it. It just happens. I can stop running or walking or climbing, but I can't stop myself from growing.

How do I know I grow? I can't feel it happening. I don't seem to be much taller today than I was last year. But the clothes I wore last year are now too small for me, and so I know I have grown. And I know the growing goes on and on.

What happens to me when I grow?

There are more than ten million million cells in my body. Each of those cells keeps getting bigger and bigger, stretching, growing. After a while each cell divides and becomes two cells. Those two cells get bigger and bigger, stretching, growing. After a time the two cells divide and become four cells. The four cells become eight cells. The dividing of my cells goes on and on.

Each day my muscles are a tiny bit bigger than they were the day before. There are more muscle cells in them. Each day my bones are a little bigger. There are more bone cells in them.

I do not have to try to grow. I just grow. And I grow at my own special speed because I am me.

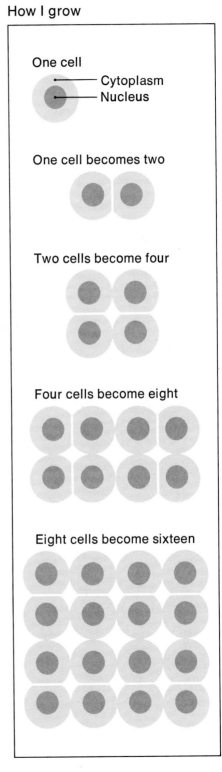

How I grow

One cell
— Cytoplasm
— Nucleus

One cell becomes two

Two cells become four

Four cells become eight

Eight cells become sixteen

My bones grow

One day my mother let me hold my baby brother. "Why is he so much softer than I am?" I asked.

My mother said, "One reason he feels softer is that his bones aren't as hard as yours are. When babies are born, they have very few hard bones. Their skeletons are mostly cartilage. But bone cells work all the time, and so bones get bigger and harder. Your bones are bigger and harder than the baby's, and my bones are bigger and harder than yours. Your bones will grow and get harder and harder until you are about twenty years old."

Once the doctor took an X ray of my wrist. The doctor wanted to see how my bones were growing. I asked how a picture of my wrist could show what was happening to all the bones in my body.

The doctor said, "Your wrist has eight bones in it. But they do not get there all at once. Some children's wrist bones grow faster or slower than the wrist bones of other children. But the wrist bones grow in the same step-by-step way in all healthy children. If your wrist bones look right on the X ray, then, most likely, the rest of your bones are also growing the way they should."

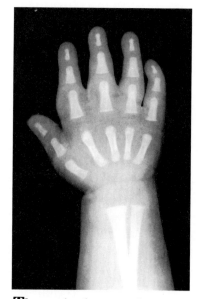

The wrist bones of a newborn baby are not very hard. They do not show on an X ray.

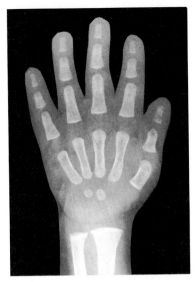

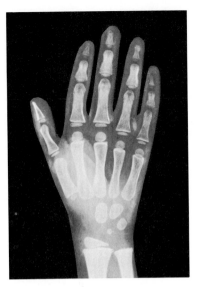

Two small round bones are the first wrist bones to show on an X ray. The child is 1 year old.

This X ray shows four wrist bones. They are those of a child who is between 3 and 4 years old.

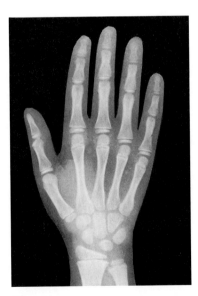

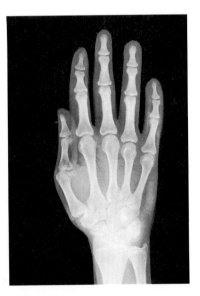

This is the wrist of a child who is 7 years old. It shows six wrist bones.

At about 17 years of age, all eight wrist bones will have grown as big, hard, and close together as they will ever be.

How big will I be?

If my cells are always dividing into new cells, why don't I grow bigger and bigger and never stop?

That won't happen! One reason is that even though my body makes new cells, other cells wear out. But there is another and more important reason I won't just keep on growing.

In my body are tiny organs called glands. Glands make things I need. I have tear glands, oil glands, sweat glands, glands that help me digest my food, glands that protect me from sickness, glands that make my heart beat faster. And I have

1 year old   3 years old   6 years old

glands that help me grow.

One gland, the pituitary gland, has charge over all the other glands. It directs them so that they work together. These glands make things that cause me to grow or stop growing.

Someday, when I'm about 20, my glands will tell my body to stop growing. Then I won't get any bigger.

When I'm grown up, my legs will be about five times as long as they were when I was a baby. My arms will be about four times as long. My head will be about two times as big.

How big will I be?

I'll be as big as ME!

Till age 11, boys and girls grow at the same speed. Then girls grow faster for a few years. But boys catch up. Most grown men are taller than most grown women.

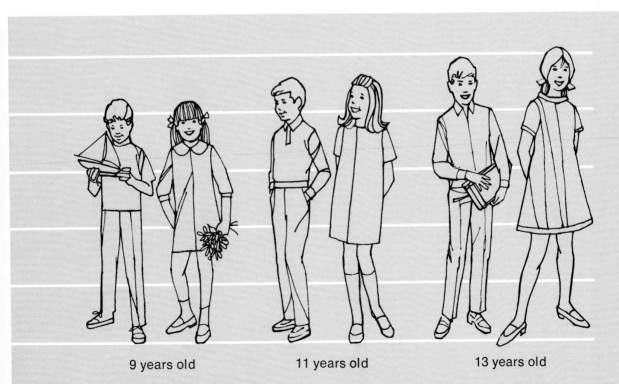

9 years old   11 years old   13 years old

Part of me is always new

As I grow, my body changes. It changes inside where I cannot see the changes. It changes outside where I can see what is happening to me.

Inside of me cells grow and divide, so I grow bigger inside as well as outside. Inside of me, cells are always growing to take the place of cells that wear out.

Outside of me something is always new. My hair grows longer. My fingernails and toenails grow, too. I lose my baby teeth, and new teeth grow in to take their place.

Before I was born, there were tiny tooth buds hidden in my gums. As I grew, my baby teeth began to form around these tooth buds. When I was about 6 months old, my first baby tooth pushed through my gums. By the time I was 3 years old, I had all 20 of my baby, or primary, teeth.

When I was about 6 years old, my first grown-up teeth were ready to come in. One by one, my grown-up, or permanent, teeth began to push my baby teeth out. When I'm older, I'll have 32 grown-up teeth. All the time, my jaws will be growing so as to make room for my bigger, grown-up teeth.

Something new is always happening to me. I am always changing.

My new teeth

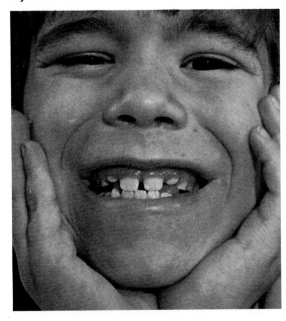

My teeth are growing

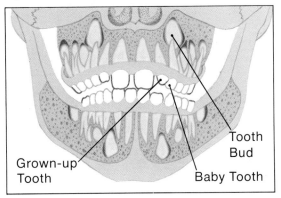

Tooth Bud

Grown-up Tooth

Baby Tooth

My teeth grow from tiny tooth buds hidden in my gums. When I lose a baby tooth, a bigger, grown-up tooth is waiting to take its place.

My body can fix itself

My body has its own way of fixing itself. It heals itself. When I hurt myself, my cells begin to do special jobs.

Suppose I cut my hand on a piece of glass. The cut place bleeds. Almost at once the blood coming from the cut begins to clot. The cells stick together. Slowly the blood gets thick and covers the cut. Then the blood gets hard. It makes kind of a cap, called a scab, over the cut.

Under the scab, other cells are working.

Germs may have got into the cut. White cells in my blood eat up the germs.

One day I cut my hand.
Blood came out of the cut.

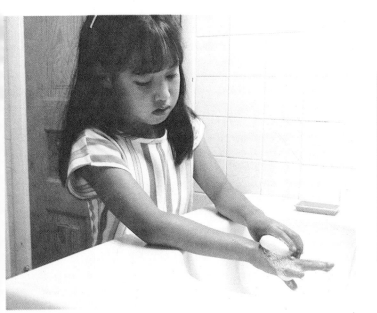

The cut wasn't deep. It didn't hurt much. I washed my hands with soap and water and then dried them on a clean towel.

Mother put a small bandage over the cut. The bandage helped keep dirt out of the cut while it was healing.

The cells along the edges of the cut grow and divide, grow and divide. New cells take the place of some of those that were hurt by the glass.

Still other cells do another kind of job. These are special healing cells. They make a kind of net that joins the edges of the cut together. Each day this net gets thicker, tougher, stronger. It is called a scar.

After a while the scab falls off my hand. Then I can see the scar.

My hand has healed itself.

Bumps, bruises, and blisters

Sometimes I bump my ankle or my leg or my elbow. The bump pushes a muscle against a bone, and tiny veins and arteries break. I have a bruise.

A bruise is a kind of an upside-down cut. When I cut myself, blood comes out of the cut. But blood does not come out of a bruise. Instead, it moves below the top layer of my skin. The blood shows through my skin as dark blue or black.

As the bruise heals, it may change color. Sometimes it changes to purple, then to lavender, then to yellow. Each color is lighter than the last. This means that the blood is moving back into my body. The bruised muscle is getting well.

One time I burned my hand on the barbecue grill. The burned spot puffed up. I had a blister. A blister is kind of a puffy little pocket in the layers of my skin. The top layer of skin pulls away from the layers under it, and the space fills with liquid. The top layer keeps germs from getting into the blister.

My cells start to do their healing job just as they do when I have a cut. Slowly the liquid moves back into my body, and my blister heals.

One day, I got in a fight with another boy and bruised my eye.

I had a blister. I was careful not to break it and let germs get in.

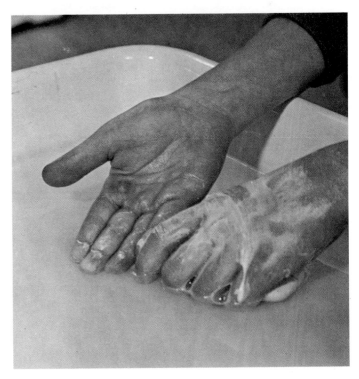

I kept my hands clean. After a while the blister healed.

Pain is a signal

Once in a while some part of me hurts. Nerves send messages to my brain. The messages say that a part of me is not well. The pain is a signal. My brain understands.

I do not like pain. But if I did not have pain, I wouldn't know that something needed fixing. When I have a pain I tell my parents or my teacher where it hurts.

Sometimes I have a pain in my stomach. Once I had a stomachache that went away when my mother gave me some medicine. But once I had a bad pain in my stomach. The doctor thought I might have appendicitis. He wanted me to have a blood count.

A laboratory technician at the hospital took a drop of my blood. People in the laboratory looked at it through a microscope. They looked to see if the numbers of red cells and white cells were correct.

My blood count was all right. That meant my appendix was all right. The doctor said maybe I had eaten too many green apples. But the pain was a signal, and I paid attention to it.

I am not a crybaby, but I sometimes cry when I hurt. Even crying can be helpful. It seems to make the pain better. And it tells people that I really hurt.

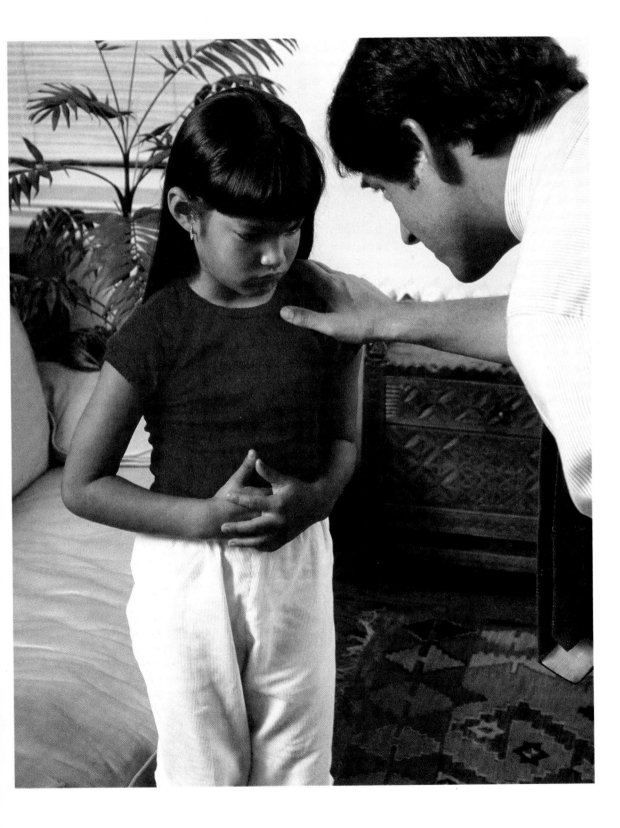

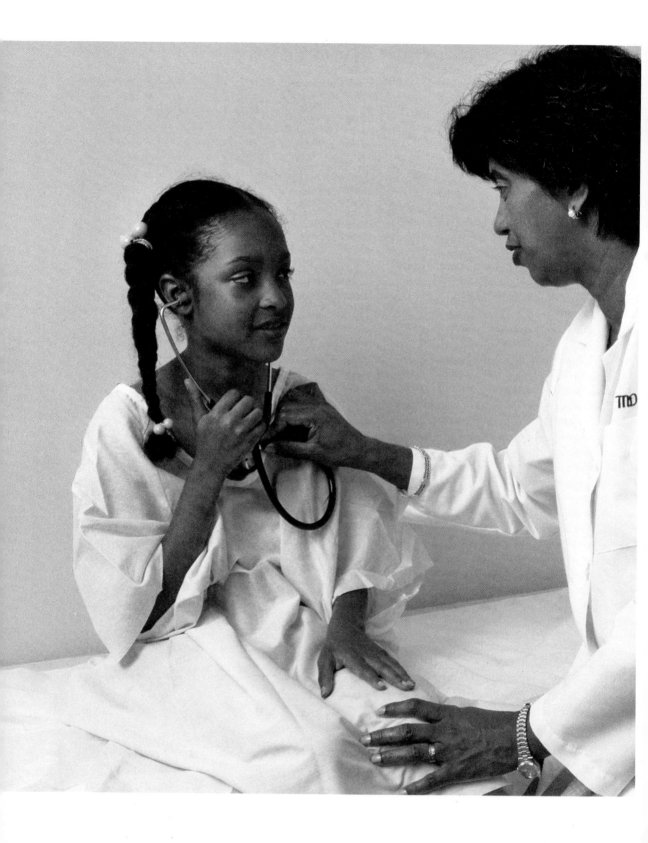

I go to the doctor

I go to the doctor when I'm sick. The doctor may give me medicine or a shot, called an injection. Germs make me sick. Medicine helps fight the germs.

But there are times when I go to the doctor and I'm not sick at all. This kind of visit is called a checkup.

The thing around the doctor's neck is called a stethoscope. The earpieces of the stethoscope fit inside the doctor's ears. The doctor uses the stethoscope to listen to sounds inside my body. Yes, my body does make some inside sounds.

The doctor holds the stethoscope up to my chest and listens to the sound of my heart beating. Sometimes the doctor lets me listen, too.

Then the doctor moves the stethoscope around on my chest to hear my breathing.

There are sounds in my stomach, and the doctor listens to these, too.

Sounds tell kind of a story of what is going on inside me. Sounds help the doctor know that I am growing up well and strong, exactly as I should.

Body sounds tell the inside story about me. But they are not the whole story. The doctor does other things, too.

The doctor shines a little light into my eyes. The light helps the doctor look into the inside of my eyes to see if they are healthy. Then I read the letters on a wall chart. The doctor wants to be sure I am seeing all I should see.

The doctor shines another light into my ears. The light helps the doctor look into many of the inside places in my ears. The doctor wants to be sure that all my ear openings are clear. If there is any sickness in my ears, I may not hear all I should hear.

Sometimes we talk about the kinds of food that are good for me. The doctor tells me to get plenty of sleep and to play outdoors a lot. I need food and sleep and fresh air to help me grow.

There is a folder in the doctor's office. It has my name on it. The doctor writes in it each time I visit. The doctor weighs me and writes down how much I weigh. The doctor measures me and writes down how tall I am. I can see if my weight and height have changed since my last visit.

If I go to the doctor when I am well, I may not get sick.

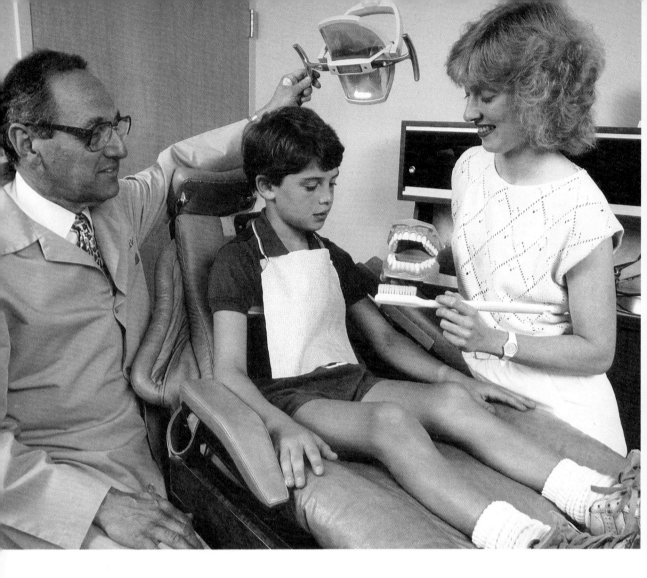

I go to the dentist

I go to the doctor when I am well so I can stay that way. And I go to the dentist when I am well so that my teeth will stay healthy.

I sit in a special chair that goes up and down. It has a headrest that the dentist moves to fit my head. It has a footrest, too.

The dentist uses small tools when working in my mouth. One tool is a little

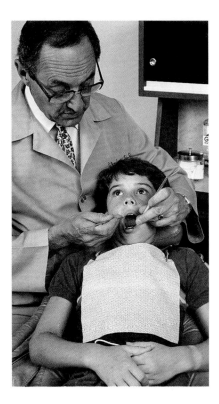

round mirror on a handle. The dentist can see the sides of my teeth with the mirror. To feel for cavities, the dentist touches each tooth with a little pick called an explorer. Cavities are little holes in my teeth, caused by germs.

The dentist has a helper, called a dental hygienist, who shows me the right way to brush and floss my teeth. The hygienist usually cleans and polishes my teeth. The dentist and the dental hygienist help my teeth stay healthy and strong.

If some of my teeth are not straight, the dentist may send me to a special dentist, called an orthodontist, who straightens teeth. The orthodontist may put braces on my teeth. Braces are little metal rings held together by thin wires. The orthodontist uses the wires to move my teeth until they are straight.

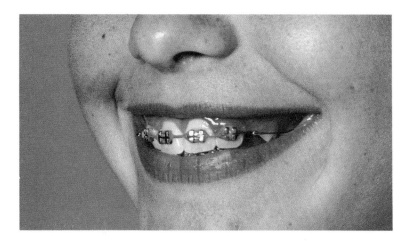

My dentist told me that germs called bacteria live on teeth. The bacteria make cavities. Once I had a cavity filled.

First the dentist used a drill. A drill is a very tiny wheel at the end of a shiny thing like a pencil. The dentist held the drill against my tooth. The tiny wheel went around very fast. It made a buzzing sound and it stung a little, and it cleaned out the cavity.

Then the dentist mixed a kind of paste called a filling. After using it to fill the cavity, the dentist rubbed it and scraped it until it was smooth and hard. Then my tooth was almost as good as new.

Once the dentist took out one of my baby teeth. My grown-up tooth was ready to come in, but my baby tooth was in the way. It wouldn't budge.

The dentist put some medicine into the skin around my tooth. It stung a little, but then my tooth had no feeling in it. The dentist moved my baby tooth back and forth. And then out it came, and it didn't even hurt. Now I have a grown-up tooth in the place where the baby tooth was.

I take care of my teeth. My grown-up teeth must last for the rest of my life.

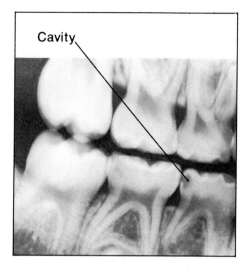

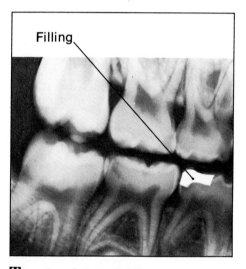

The dentist took X-ray pictures of my teeth. One picture showed that I had a cavity. First the dentist cleaned out the cavity, then filled it. Now my teeth are fine.

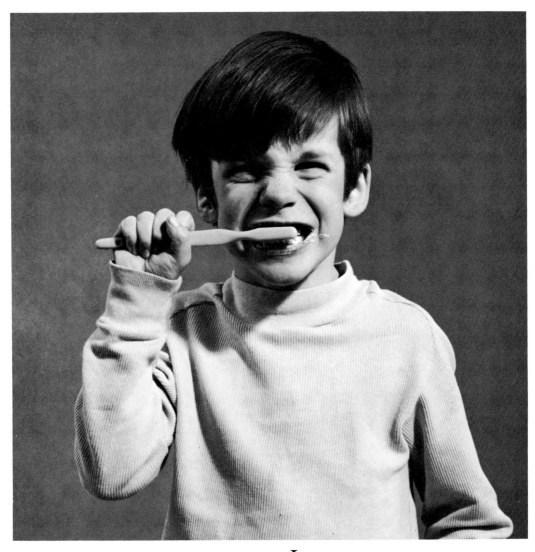

I use my toothbrush to get rid of bits of food that may stick to my teeth. I put some toothpaste on the brush and move it up and down over my teeth. I brush the back as well as the front of my teeth.

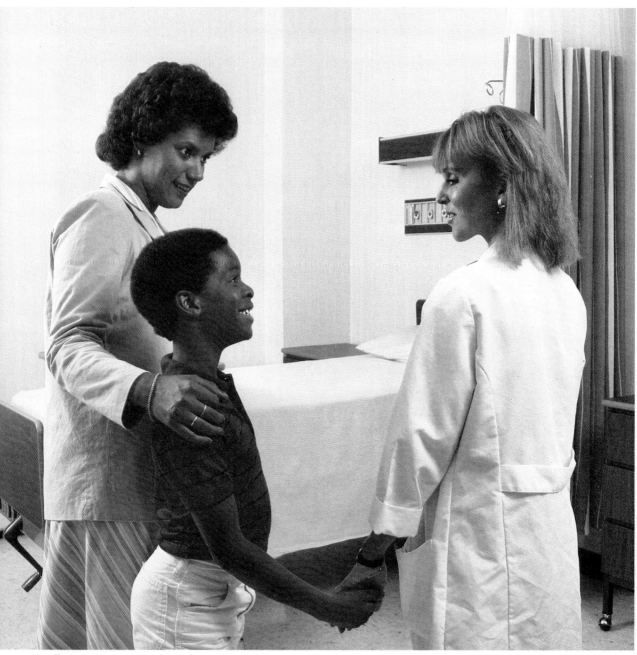

I go to the hospital. I am
worried. Then a nurse comes. She
holds out her hand and smiles at
me. I feel better.

I go to the hospital

Once, when I was sick I had to go to the hospital. I stayed there for a while.

Hospitals sound different from my house. There is the sound of wheels. Meal carts and wheel chairs and scrub pails roll on wheels. Nurses' shoes make soft padding sounds. Mothers' heels make tap-tapping sounds. A soft voice somewhere says, "Calling Dr. Brown." One sound I always like to hear is dishes rattling. That means it's time to eat!

Hospitals smell different from my house, too. They smell of soap and floor polish and the cream the nurse rubs on my back. Sometimes they smell of medicine. Sometimes I smell flowers.

Hospitals are kept very, very clean. People who work in hospitals must be clean, too. Nurses and doctors wash their hands many times a day. I have to wash myself often, too, when I'm in the hospital.

My hospital bed has sides on it. They go up and down. A card at the end of my bed has my name on it. I wear a bracelet with my name on it, too. And I wear a hospital gown in the hospital.

Hospitals have a great many special people who do their best to help me get well. The helpers I see most are the nurses and nurses' aides. The nurses take care of

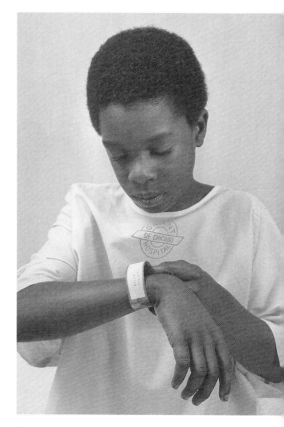

I put on a hospital gown. Then a nurse gives me a bracelet that has my name on it.

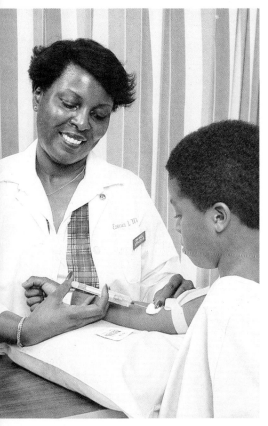

A laboratory technician takes a little of my blood. It will help the doctor to help me.

me by doing what my doctor says. The aides help the nurses in every way they can.

Sometimes my doctor does not want me to get out of bed. Then a nurse or an aide may help me to eat or even to take a bath right in bed.

Sometimes my doctor wants an X ray. An X ray is a picture of some part of the inside of me. The X-ray technologist takes an X ray with a giant-sized camera.

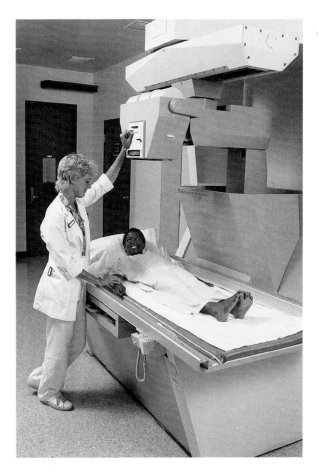

In a special room, an X-ray technologist takes a picture of me—an X ray. It doesn't hurt.

There is a special place where I can play when I am feeling better.

Blood tells many things about my body. A laboratory technician takes a little blood from my arm or a fingertip. She uses a needle. It stings, but it isn't bad. Blood tests help the doctor know how to take care of me.

Many other people help me when I am in the hospital, too.

People from the play department teach me new things to do that are fun.

Teachers come to help children study.

I do what the hospital helpers want me to do. I want to get well and go home.

I can take a toy with me to the hospital. My mother and father can visit me every day. I watch television. I make new friends. Time goes quickly. I get well. And then I go home.

I was sick. Now I'm well. Good-by, hospital. Good-by, new friends. Good-by, Doctor. Hello, Mother!

The doctor felt my arm. It hurt. "She must have an X ray," the doctor said.

A technician put a bandage on my arm. Then he put wet plaster over the bandage. The plaster dried into a cast that kept my arm still until it healed.

I go to the emergency room

If I get very sick all of a sudden or if I have an accident, I go to the emergency room of the hospital.

Nurses and doctors in the emergency room work quickly. They don't talk much. They may even seem unfriendly at first. But they are just very busy. They know the best way to take care of me.

If I have swallowed something bad they must work fast to get it out. If I have cut myself, they must stop the bleeding. The cut must be cleaned and fixed. If I have had a bad fall I must be checked for broken bones.

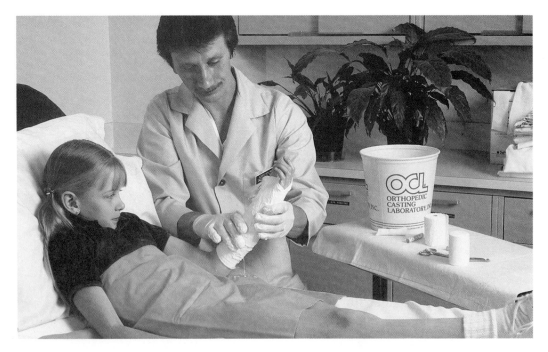

The doctor may need an X ray to see if something inside of me was hurt. I may have to have my leg or arm put in a cast. A cast is made of plaster. It is stiff and keeps my broken bone from moving until it is well.

Sometimes there are other patients in the emergency room besides me. The nurses and doctors must take care of all of them.

The lights are very bright. I hear water running and metal clinking and people talking in low voices. Sometimes I hear someone crying.

When I am all fixed up I say good-by to the nurses and doctors. I thank them for helping me. Then I go home.

The doctor showed me my X ray. I could see where the bone was broken.

It was fun asking my friends to write on my cast. After the doctor took the cast off, my arm felt a lot better.

I Wonder, I Think

Wondering me

I wonder, wonder, wonder, all day long. My dad says I'm a "wonder machine."

I wonder how my dog knows I'm home from school even before I open the door.

I wonder about people. Why are some people left-handed?

I wonder about myself.

I wonder why I yawn.

I wonder . . . both food and air enter my mouth. How does my throat know where to send food, where to send air?

I wonder why I hiccup.

I wonder why cutting my hair and nails doesn't hurt.

I wonder why the "funny bone" in my elbow tingles.

I live in a wonder-filled world. There is much for me to wonder about.

I can wonder only because I have a mind, because I can think.

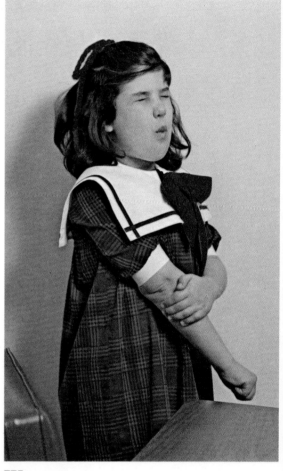

Why does my "funny bone" tingle?

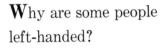Why are some people
left-handed?

How does my throat
know where to send food
and where to send air?

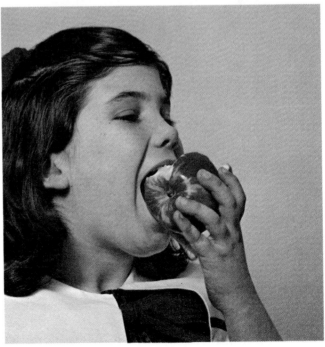

Answers for me

I wonder and I find the answers.

Dogs have extra-sharp hearing. My dog knows me by my footsteps.

Some people are left-handed because the part of their brain that directs their left hand is stronger than the part that directs their right hand.

I yawn because I'm sleepy. The great gulps of air bring extra oxygen into my body. Then I feel more wide awake.

When I swallow, a little lid called the epiglottis closes over my trachea. Food slides past my trachea and into my stomach.

Here's why I have hiccups. My dia-phragm jerks, pulling air into my lungs. If my epiglottis is closed, the air smacks into it. This moves my vocal cords, and a *hic* sound comes out.

Cutting my hair and nails doesn't hurt because there are no nerves in my hair and nails. I feel pain only in those parts of my body where I have nerves.

My "funny bone" is really a "funny nerve." This nerve lies close to the surface near my elbow. When I bump it, the nerve is touched. I feel the tingles right down to my fingertips.

I understand answers to my questions because I have a mind.

I learn by looking. That's how I know that caterpillars have feelers to guide them when they crawl.

Sometimes when I'm shopping I see things that puzzle me. I ask about them. That's another way to learn.

I know about places, people, and things I've never seen because I've read about them.

What's right? What's wrong?

I wonder about other kinds of things, too. I wonder:

Why was I made?

What am I on earth for?

What does being alive mean?

What makes me think?

What makes me feel?

How do I know what is right?

IIow do I know what is wrong?

Why do I do what I do when I do it?

How do I decide to do what I do?

These are very hard things to wonder about. They are too hard to think about all by myself. I need to know more things than I can find in books.

What do I do?

I ask my father and mother about things like this. We talk about them. We try to find answers together.

My dad says that hunting for answers to questions like these can help me know myself. He says I won't find all the answers all at once, but I will find the beginnings of answers that will grow as I grow and guide me in everything I do.

Even though I can't always understand all of the answers to hard questions, I'm glad I have a mind that wonders and thinks and hunts for answers.

Thinking

I have been wondering. That's thinking.

I found some answers. I read them and understood them. That's thinking, too.

Scientists don't know exactly how people think. They do know that people think with their brains. And they know some of the kinds of thinking people do.

I remember. That's thinking. I remember my last birthday . . . what I learned in school last year . . . what time I must be home for dinner.

I can think about things that are just ideas. That's another kind of thinking. I know what the number 10 means. I know what loving my mother and father means.

I decide about things. I look at two pictures I have made and I say, "This one is better." That's thinking.

I plan and make things—a model, a puppet. I have to think to do that.

I wonder, remember, decide, plan, understand ideas. I think. And I do it all with my brain.

The human brain weighs only about three pounds (1.5 kilograms). A six-year-old child's brain is as big as a grown-up's brain. The brain isn't large, but it's important. I learn, remember, and think with my brain.

An electronic "brain" is huge. A human brain is small. Yet an electronic "brain" can't do anything unless human brains help it.

I can think of different ways to show that I know what *10* means.

Do animals think?

I saw a robin build a nest.

The robin did not have to learn how to build a nest. It knew from the time it was born. This knowing is called instinct. Even if a robin never saw a nest, it would make the kind of nest robins have made for thousands of years.

My cat had kittens.

She took good care of the kittens. She washed them and fed them and carried them by holding the fur on their necks in her mouth. My cat took care of her kittens just as cats have always done. She knew how to care for her kittens because of instinct.

Robins, cats, and other animals do many things because of instinct.

But some animals can learn to do things that aren't instinctive.

I taught my dog to sit up and beg. When I went to the circus, I saw a tiger jump through a hoop. The tiger's trainer taught

A cat takes care of her kittens in the same way that cats have always cared for their kittens. A cat knows how to take care of kittens because of instinct.

it to do that. My friend taught his parakeet to say "Hello," "Good-by," and "Go to school."

Some animals can think enough to solve problems, too.

Scientists prove this with experiments. A scientist may put a hungry monkey in a cage and give the monkey a stick. Then, the scientist puts some food outside the cage. The monkey sees the food and wants it. First, the monkey tries to get the food by sticking its arm between the bars of the cage. But, it can't reach the food. The food is too far away. After a while, the monkey grabs the stick and uses it to pull the food into the cage. The monkey has solved a problem by itself.

Animals have instinct. Some can learn simple tricks. And some can think enough to solve problems. But animals can't think as well as people do. I am smarter than any animal.

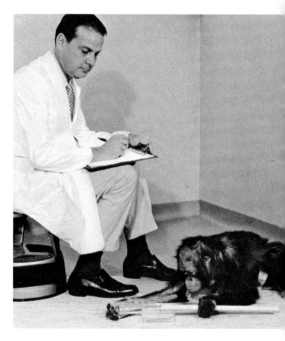

This orangutan is trying to get a piece of food out of the plastic tube. To solve the problem, he pushes the rod through the tube. His reward for thinking? A snack.

Knowledge

An animal knows some things by instinct. Some animals learn things, such as how to get food, from their parents. But no animal can think up *new* ideas and teach these ideas to other animals. That's something only people can do.

Very long ago, people didn't use numbers. But when they began to keep herds of sheep and cows, they had to be able to count their animals. So people thought of numbers. This was a new idea. People taught their children about numbers, and in this way they passed the idea along.

Once, there was no such thing as writing. Then, people thought of the alphabet. This was a new idea, one they could teach to others.

All through history, people have thought of new ideas and new ways to do things. Paper on which to write. Printing presses for printing books. Television to send pictures into my home. Computers that quickly solve problems that would take people years to work out. Machines to do all kinds of work.

All these ideas have been passed along from the people of one time to people born long after them.

I am a person. I can learn from all the

millions of people who have lived before me. All their ideas and thinking have been passed along to me. That's knowledge. And knowledge is one of the greatest of all gifts.

I Speak, I Listen

My voice comes from a box

If I say "fee-fi-fo-fum," I can feel the place where my voice comes from. I put my fingers on my throat and I can feel my throat moving.

My voice comes from my voice box, called a larynx. My voice box is in the middle of my throat. In it are tiny muscles called vocal cords.

Breath from my lungs makes my vocal cords move. When they move fast, they make a sound. I can see how this works by blowing up a balloon, then pinching the neck. When I let the air out through the neck, it moves and makes a sound.

As soon as I was born I could make sounds. Air from my lungs moved my vocal cords when I laughed or cried. People understood what those sounds meant. But I couldn't talk.

As I grew, I found that I could use my nose, tongue, teeth, and lips to help make different kinds of sounds. I said *muh, duh,* and *eee.* I began to copy the sounds of people around me. I put the sounds together to make words like *mama, daddy,* and *mine.*

As I got bigger, I learned bigger words— *penny, grandma, surprise,* and *chipmunk.* Now I can say words like *elephant* and *television* and *astronaut.*

Air helps me speak

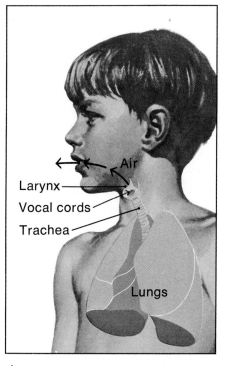

Air goes from my lungs, through my trachea, and into my larynx. In the larynx, the air moves my vocal cords back and forth and makes sounds.

A person who is partly deaf may not hear
all the sounds in every word. Because
he says words the way he hears them,
he may need help to learn to speak
correctly. Some speech teachers have
a child look into a mirror while he
talks so that he can see his mouth as
it forms the proper sounds.

今日は
kon
nichi
wa
(Japanese)

你好吗
nai
hao
ma
(Chinese)

ЗДРАВСТВУЙТЕ
Zdrav st voo ee tee eh
(Russian)

pĺơe
shalom
(Hebrew)

万 Lo ன் ஃ π 刀 Lஂ
na ma s ka ra m
(Tamil—Sri Lanka)

زيك صحّ
zayak sahha
(Arabic)

नमस्ते
na ma stè
(Hindi—India)

Hola, allo, hello

I need words for lots of things—to say who I am . . . to talk to my friends . . . to tell funny stories . . . to ask directions . . . to shout, "Happy Birthday!" . . . to call my mother . . . to whisper a secret.

The words I use are American English words. But many of these words had their beginnings in other countries—in Spain or Germany or France or Italy.

Some of my words came from the German people. *Pretzel, noodle,* and *kindergarten* are a few of these words.

Balloon is a word that came to me from the Italian people.

I know some words that were invented in the United States—*jeep, hot dog, fizzle, cowboy,* and *bulldozer.* Some of my American English words even came to me from the first Americans, the Indians—words like *tepee, moccasin, pecan,* and *raccoon.*

I know some words that sound a little alike in different languages. Some have the same meaning, too. If I spoke Spanish I would say *hola.* If I spoke French I would say *allo.* But I speak English and I say *hello. Hola . . . allo . . . hello*—whichever way I say it, it means the same thing.

I use the English language, and so do people in Great Britain, Canada, Australia, New Zealand, and some other countries. But American English and British English aren't always the same. American children and British children often have different names for the same things. Here are some examples.

The American Way		The British Way
cookies	are	biscuits
a baby buggy	is	a pram
gasoline	is	petrol
a washcloth	is	a face flannel
a radio	is	a wireless
an elevator	is	a lift
the subway	is	the underground
a sweater	is	a jersey
oatmeal	is	porridge
candies	are	sweets
a vacation	is	a holiday
good-by	is	cheerio

I play with sounds

I use words to say the things I want to say. But sometimes I like to play with words and sounds and sayings.

If I say "Shhh," "Ooops," "Ugh," "Hiss," or "Buzz," I wonder—"Is that a sound I'm saying with a word, or a word I'm saying with a sound?"

I puzzle over the funny way words can be used, and I ask myself:

"Windows have panes, but do they hurt?"

"If I go up the street, must I always come back down?"

"If I straighten a room, will it curl up when I leave?"

"Can I really be an early bird?"

"Why doesn't our fir tree grow coats?"

I like to say words that curl my tongue —*silly, pillow, wallop.* I think it's fun to use *thingamajig* and *whatchamacallit* words. And I like to twist words around, like this: wiggle waggle, jiggle jaggle, diggle daggle, higgeldy piggeldy, humpedy dumpedy stumpedy.

I have words to say what I need to say, words to puzzle over and play with, words to laugh and think about. I like to use words. I like to talk.

Aitch-choo! That's how I think a
sneeze sounds. I listen to sounds
and I try to copy them. Sometimes I
play a game. I make a list of sounds
I've heard. Then I try to match the
sounds to pictures I see in books.

Try to match the list of sounds to the pictures.

a. bow-wow   f. hiss
b. whack   g. buzz
c. plunk   h. cheep
d. tweet   i. jingle-jingle
e. whoosh   j. boom

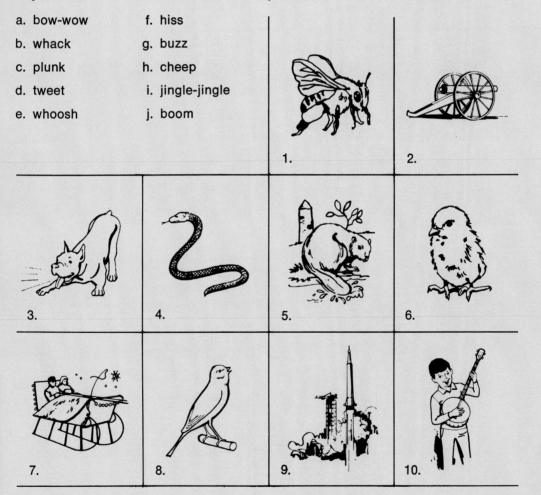

Answers: 1g, 2j, 3a, 4f, 5b, 6h, 7i, 8d, 9e, 10c

Learning to listen

My ears can hear dozens—maybe even hundreds—of sounds all at the same time. All around me are the sounds of animals, things, nature, and people. If I really heard all these sounds at the same time, I would be very mixed up. So I don't just hear—I listen. Unless it's too noisy, my brain picks out the sounds I need.

I listen to the people and the things that interest me—my dad telling a story . . . my favorite TV program.

I listen to sounds that are a little spooky—the basement stairs creaking . . . wind in the trees.

I listen to popcorn popping or the cat purring, and these sounds give me a warm feeling.

I listen to warnings—"Watch out for the ball!"

I listen to instructions—how to play a game . . . how to put together a puzzle.

I listen to orders from grown-ups—"It's time to go to bed!"

When my brain chooses what my ears will hear, then I think and I feel and I know I am listening.

I listen in special ways

Sometimes special instruments help me listen. There are instruments that copy sounds on records or tapes, and I can listen to these sounds over and over again. There are instruments that make sounds louder so that I am able to hear them. And there are instruments that send sounds through wires or through the air so that they reach me from faraway places.

Once I talked into the microphone on a tape recorder. Then I listened to my voice talking back to me.

Once I put on the doctor's stethoscope, and I listened to my own heart beating.

On holidays I listen to my grandma talking to me on the telephone. Her voice comes to me from far away.

I watched the astronauts on television. They were way up in space, but I listened to them talk.

Almost every day at school, I listen to the principal speak on the intercom.

Listening to sounds and voices that come to me through special instruments helps me learn about the world in which I live.

In Australia, some children live so far from school they learn their lessons by special radio.

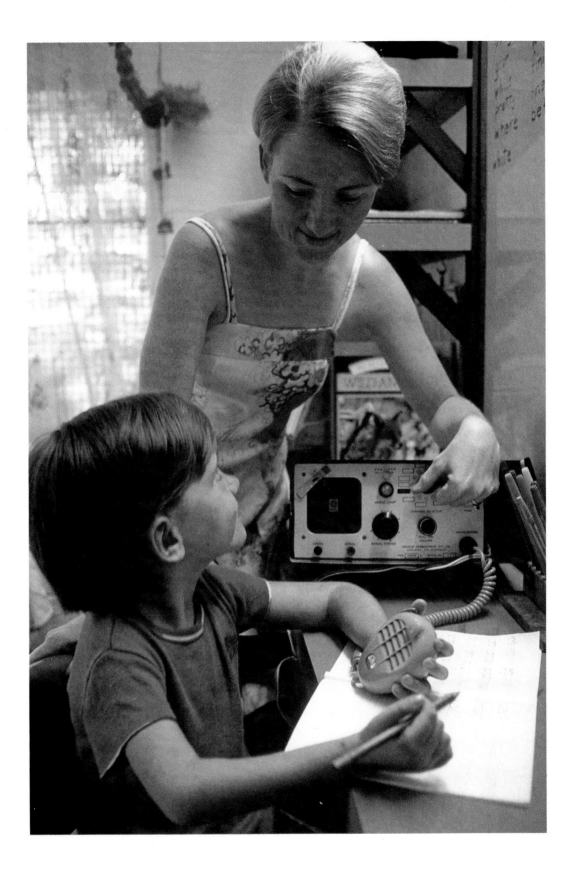

I see signs

Sometimes there is so much noise I cannot hear words. Or sometimes people are too far away for their voices to reach me. But they make signs with their arms and hands and I know what the signs mean.

In downtown traffic a policeman holds up his hand. That means our car must stop.

In the baseball park the umpire makes a sign with his thumb and fist. This tells me that a player is out.

At a concert the band leader raises his baton high, and I know the musicians are ready to play.

Some actions say things almost better than words can.

I saw soldiers salute when the flag passed by. I knew what the salute meant.

I clapped hard when a magician came to our school and did tricks for us. The magician bowed. That meant, "Thank you."

Sometimes just the looks on peoples' faces tell me something I need to know.

Yesterday when my friends and I went running through our living room, I saw Dad put down his newspaper. He wrinkled his forehead and pressed his lips together. I knew what that meant—Dad was cross. We quieted down. Then he smiled.

I can hear, but sometimes I use my eyes to "listen." Deaf people always "listen" with their eyes. They learn to use their hands and fingers to make signs that spell words. They "speak" with their hands and see what others say.

Most of me talks

Every day in some way I use my arms and hands and head or other parts of my body to help me say things.

When the baby is sleeping I hold my finger to my lips. That means, "Quiet, please."

In school I raise my hand so the teacher knows I am asking for a turn to speak.

I place my hand over my heart when I want to show I care about our country's flag.

Riding my bicycle, I let people in cars or walking on the sidewalk know I am going to turn. I signal with my arm.

I like to make the all-okay sign for my friends.

Once in a while I feel shy. It's hard to answer questions. But I can say "Yes" or "No" by nodding or shaking my head. If I shrug my shoulders, that means, "I don't know," or "MM—well—maybe."

Sometimes I just feel like being quiet. That can mean something, too.

And that's why I say that most of me talks.

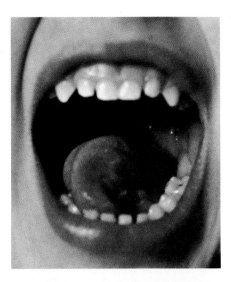

Speaking, listening, watching

I speak in many ways. I speak with words most of the time. But sometimes I just speak with sounds that aren't words. And sometimes I let my actions speak for me.

I don't just hear—I listen. My brain chooses what I will hear. And sometimes my eyes help me understand a message.

Speaking, listening, and watching— these are three of the ways I learn about my world and the people in it.

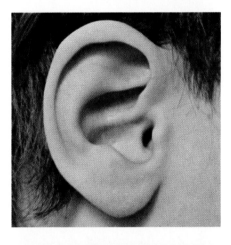

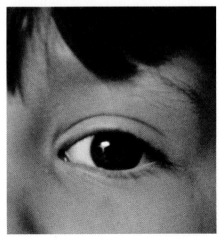

What I Can Do

I can pretend

In one single day or even in an hour, I can pretend to be as many me's as I want to be. I can pretend to be a movie star, an artist, a teacher, a doctor, an inventor. I can pretend that I am anywhere at any time doing anything I want to do. I can go back to long ago. I can go ahead into a time that has yet to come. I can "see" all this in the world inside my mind.

When I tell my mother about my different me's and the things they do and the places they go, she smiles and says, "You have imagination." That's what she calls pretending.

Now I work with maps that other people have made. But I dream of the day when I will help to make a map.

She says that children aren't the only ones who pretend. Grown-ups do it, too. Someone must "see" a thing in a pretend world before it can be made into a part of the real world. How else could there be new things that never were before?

Without imagination there would be no rocket ships, airplanes, telephones, television, or the many other things I see in my world. No one could make up a poem or a story. No one could make beautiful paintings or statues.

I learn when inventors, artists, writers, and others share with me the worlds they "see" inside their minds. I want to share my pretend world, too.

I pretend that I can build roads. Grown-ups pretend, too. They build models for things in the real world.

I wonder and I wish

I wonder if I'll ever know about everything in my world. I ask about the things that puzzle me. I learn some new thing every day. Still I wonder.

I write poems that tell about the things that are important to me. I write about the things that make me laugh when I think of them. Thoughtful or funny, each poem I write tells something about me.

I Wish I Were
I wish I were a baseball cap
And lived on someone's head.
Naaa, that's no good 'cause they would
Leave me when they went to bed.

I wish I were a shining star
To give the people light.
Naaa, that wouldn't be much better
'Cause I'd only live at night.

I wish I were an engine
That lived behind a hood.
Naaa, I don't think that would work
'Cause gas doesn't taste that good.

I'm glad I'm not a baseball cap,
A car, a bird, a toy.
There's only one thing I'm thankful for,
And that's that I'm a boy!

Scott Fleming, Age 9,
California

I Wish I Were a Fish

I wish I were a fish;
   Then I'd stay clean all day.
I wouldn't have to take a bath.
   I'd swim the sand away.

     Richard Gowenlock, Age 8,
     California

I wonder why the world is round,
And why some people always frown.

Why is ice cream freezing cold?
Why are lions fearless and bold?

Why are some people so shy?
Why is it good to have blueberry pie?

These are the things I
wonder why.

     Diane Zeleny, Age 9,
     Illinois

People I know

I like to pretend what it would be like to have lived long ago. It's fun to think how the world will be a hundred years from now. But I'd rather be alive in my world right now. It is the place where the people I know and love live.

Me

Lisa Jeanne is my name,
When my brother's naughty, I get the blame.

Lisa Pieta, Age 6,
New York

The Grown-ups

Sometimes I go out for lunch with the grown-ups.
I am always near grown-ups. They are my friends.
My friends are nice.

Gretchen Steig, Age 6,
Texas

I know a lady who's 80.
I like that lady and she likes to be 80.

I'm 8 and it's great
To be 8
And I like it, too.

Nancy Nemecek, Age 7,
Texas

My Uncle Jack

My Uncle Jack collects door knobs;
Door knobs here, door knobs there
Door knobs simply everywhere;
Six on the window, twelve on the door
There's hardly room for any more;
Door knobs on the light switch and on the wall,
My Uncle Jack has got them all;
Blue ones, green ones, yellow ones and red
And a row of gray ones on the bottom of his bed.

David Amey, Age 10,
England

Boys,
Smart, sensible,
Play, eat, sleep,
Considerate of others,
Boys.

Jay Foggy, Age 9,
Wisconsin

A drawing by Elizabeth Lupfer,
Age 9, Illinois

Papier-mâché dolls by
Betty Shimoda, Age 11,
Alice Shimoda, Age 9,
Illinois

Outside my door

I never used to think of things like rain, snow, trees, or flowers. They were just a part of the world outside my door.

Now I go for a walk and I see things I never saw before. I see the shapes that shadows make and the changing color of leaves. And sometimes things I look at remind me of things quite different from the things I see. Rain reminds me of falling tears. Snow makes me think of feathers floating through the air.

The Seasons

Spring is nice,
Winter has ice.
Fall is gold,
Summer is bold.

> Linda Danber, Age 7,
> Illinois

Two Little Clouds

Two little clouds were sitting in the sky.
The wind came along and then they both cried
—then it rained!

> David McCoy, Age 6,
> New York

Thunder

I hear
the drummers
strike
the sky.

> Glenys Van Every, Age 9,
> Australia

Snow is like a feather covering the whole world.

> Tim Wold, Age 6,
> Wisconsin

A painting by Serena Bedendo,
Age 7, Italy

Folded paper cutout

My senses

My world is filled with sights, sounds, smells, and things to touch or taste. My eyes, ears, fingers, nose, and mouth help me to choose the things I like.

Sometimes I ask myself questions, "Why do I like to eat an apple? Why do I like to look at the sea?"

And then I write a poem to see if I can answer me.

Apples

Apples are sour,
Apples are sweet.
Apples are juicy
And nice to eat!

Kenneth Pedersen, Age 8,
Wisconsin

Soft Noises

I like soft noises.
The sound of the wind blowing
People walking on tiptoes
And of people breathing
When they sleep or doze.

Karen Warren, Age 8,
Texas

I Love To Touch

I like to touch flowers
Because they feel like ivory showers,
They feel so soft and tender,
They are very nice,
They are white as mice
Or pink as roses,
Or maybe even green as hoses.
No matter what color,
I will always like the way they are.

Erhard Dinda, Age 9,
Wisconsin

God

Thank you, God, for making me.
And thank you for the big brown tree.
Thank you for the shining sea.
Thank you for my eyes to see.

Karen Martin, Age 7,
New York

Flowers

Flowers smell sweet.
They don't have feet
They have faces,
Hanging out of their vases.

Patricia Group, Age 7,
New York

I like animals

They creep, they crawl, they leap, they fly. They make strange noises. That's why I like to watch and listen to animals. I like the look of soft, smooth fur and shiny feathers.

Sometimes I try to copy the sounds of animals, or I try to move the way animals move. I write poems and paint pictures to tell how animals look to me.

The Runaway Tiger

Once upon a time in the middle of the night (about 12:00) a little tiger ran away because his mother had said "shut up" to him.

They lived in the forest where hardly any trees grew, but he ran away and got lost.

Fortunately his mother found out in the morning. She went out and looked for him. She hunted all morning (6:45 to 12:00) and three hours again in the afternoon. Finally she found him curled up in a pile of leaves! She said she was sorry and he said he was sorry, too. They both said they loved each other and they lived happily ever after.

Charles McDermott, Age 8,
Illinois

Caterpillar

Soft and furry,
Never in a hurry.

Stacey Cortwright, Age 8,
Illinois

The Long Snake

I have a snake
That's long and greenish.
When I pick him up
I get all squeamish.

Gregory Cooper, Age 9,
New York

Beautiful peacocks!
Beautiful cardinals!
Beautiful red wings!
I love them all.

Lisa Heron, Age 6,
Wisconsin

Some birds are yellow,
And some birds are white.
Big birds are heavy,
Little ones are light.

Some birds fly fast,
Some birds fly slow.
Others don't fly,
They just stay low.

Easter Miller, Age 9,
Texas

A paper costume by
Jennifer Stebbing, Age 9,
Illinois

A painting by Ryoto Tamai,
Age 4, Japan

I make believe

I think of things I know and see. I also think of things as they might be. Suppose I write a poem about an animal, half-elephant and half-giraffe. Shall I call it an *elephaffe?* How would it look? What would it do?

I look at things. Then, in my mind, I take them apart and put them together in new and wonderful ways. Sometimes I write poems or paint pictures to show how things might be. I make believe.

The Snapterouse

There's a snapterouse
Destroying my house,
And it's eating my garden, too.
Eating things pink, green, and blue,
Every color in the world,
Eating things straight and curled.
This is ridiculous.

He's pulled off the drapes
And eaten the grapes
And is chewing on bedcovers, too.
He has an extraordinary menu.
My house is bare.
He hasn't left a chair;
I can't sit down anywhere.

There's not a table
That's left very stable.
The foundation he's come to,
And there's nothing I can do.
My house is a mess.
You don't need the address;
You can see the destruction for miles.

I must stop this poem,
For I'll have to be goin'.
'Cause the snapterouse,
After eating my house,
Is just about to eat me!

Clare Bronowski, Age 9,
California

The star talked to the moon and they laughed
and laughed. And they kissed.

Terrie Leong, Age 7,
California

Papier-mâché masks by
Valerie Lobb, Age 9,
Denise Masanek, Age 9,
Gail Williamson, Age 9,
Illinois

A painting by Jill Susan Dobkin,
Age 10, Illinois

I play

I play games with my friends. I jump, I run, I climb, I slide. I laugh. I shout. It feels so good!

Once in a while I like to play by myself. I play with my jigsaw puzzle. I read a book. I make things. I even make up rhymes and draw pictures that tell about the things I do when I play.

Fun

Fun is being wet,
Or having a pet.
Fun is a tool,
Or staying home from school.

Fun is a game,
Or finding friends' marks the same.
Fun is laughing with glee,
Or else climbing a tree.

Fun is a cake
That your mother had to make.
Fun is a park;
Fun is a lark.

Fun can be lots of things,
Especially spring.
So don't be sad;
Be GLAD.

Jean LeBlanc, Age 8,
Wisconsin

Snowball

I had a little snowball,
It was so round and white.
I made it out of paper
So I could keep it overnight.

Tommy Meredith, Age 8,
Wisconsin

My Boat

Ker-plunk!
It sunk.
Bubble-bubble,
I'm in trouble!

Carol Ruben, Age 7,
New York

My Kite

I flew my kite in the breeze.
And it went over the trees.
I held my kite
And it went way up in its flight.

Nishan Akgulian, Age 6,
Wisconsin

A painting by Mette Olsen,
Age 10, Norway

Creative play

My feelings

How shall I tell someone what makes me happy? Or what makes me sad?

I'll make up a poem. I'll choose from all the words I know, the ones that tell exactly how I feel. I'll put them side by side in rows. Then anyone can read or say their singing sounds aloud.

My Feelings

I am fainty,
   I am fizzy,
      I am floppy.

Paul Thompson, Age 6,
New Zealand

Home

Home is a place in which to be loved,
Cared for, and understood.
Home is a place in which you talk
To your family and sisters and brothers.

Home is where, when you don't understand,
You can talk it over with your family.
Home is loving and
Loving is home.

Maureen True, Age 8,
California

Sadness

You are sad when you are lonely.
You are sad when you have no one to talk to.
You are sad when no one likes you.

David Schlotzhauer, Age 7,
New York

Crying For Food

Stop! Stop! Stop crying!
Oh boy, what a noise!
Why are they crying?
They are crying all morning,
Just crying and crying.
I just can't do anything.
I do very funny things
To make them stop crying.
But still crying, crying,
Just can't make them stop.
They are hungry.

Fred Tow, Age 9,
California

Happiness

Happiness is that good feeling,
When somebody inside
Pulls that magic string
And things start brightening.
The church bells ring.
Children sing.
That's what happiness is!

Alayne Dean, Age 9,
New York

A painting by Jed Kreinberg,
Age 9, Illinois

The Many Me's

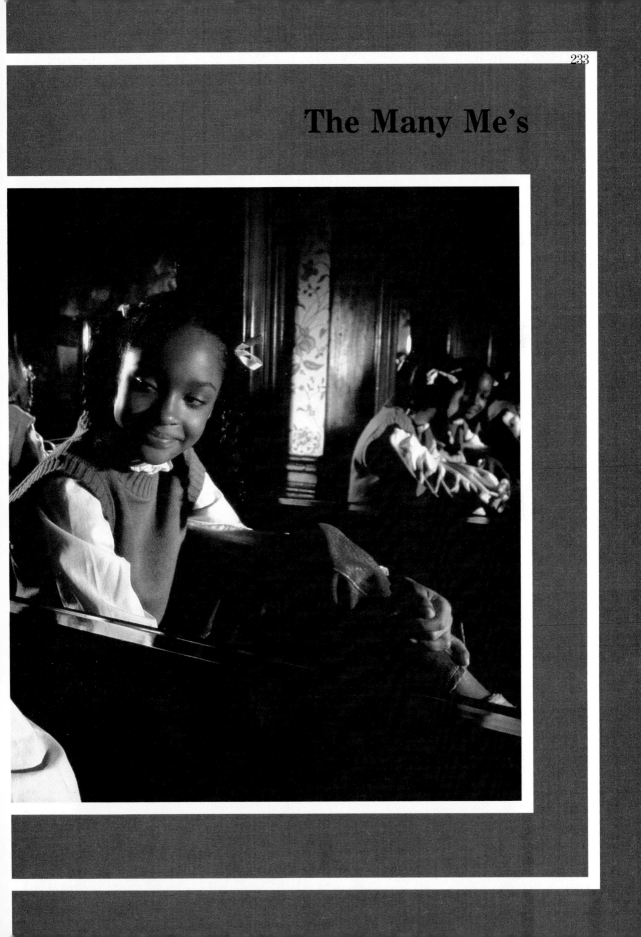

Watch me! Watch me! Watch me!

Watch me run . . . skip . . . play . . .

hop around in this cold,
cold spray!

Watch me make these pigeons fly . . .

make the earth trade places
  with sky!

I ride . . . the wind sings . . .

I'm in charge of things
  in my world.
  Oh, watch me!

The outdoor me

Whether it's rocks, leaves, sand, or snow,
I know just where I want it to go.
I play outdoors and I arrange
all sorts of things that later I'll change.
Why? Well, I like to be
part of the outdoor world, you see.

There's no one to play with

I'm all alone. There's no one around.
But I don't mind because I've found
there are lots of things to do
that are better for one than two:
Drawing, reading, thinking, dreaming
are a few.

About loving

There's Grandma, Grandpa, Dad and Mother,
special grown-ups . . .

my sister . . . my brother . . .

my doll . . . my bike . . .
my brand-new shoes . . .

a very best friend I choose . . .

helpless creatures, soft and small—
I love them all!

Sometimes I'm angry

Fight?
I might.
I'm angry, not thinking straight.
The smart thing to do would be to wait
till I cool off, and so does he.
Then we can talk of what's bothering me.

Sometimes I'm afraid

Mother was lost. Where was she?
Around the corner, looking for me!
So many things I used to fear—
storms . . . dreams . . . the dark—last year.
But time has passed. I've grown taller,
while those fears of mine have grown
  lots smaller.
Tell me: Will the things I fear today
by next year all have gone away?

Sometimes I'm sad

Things are all mixed up and I
can't think of a thing to do but cry.

Go away, you tears! I'd rather smile.
And I just might—in a little while.

I feel sort of quiet and sad.
I wish, oh I wish, I hadn't got mad.
I'll say I'm sorry, make things right,
and I'll never-never-never have another
  fight.

I said a mean thing. My pup won't play.
Grandma went home. It's been
  an awful day!
Tomorrow will be better, that I know.
How? Because I'll make it so!

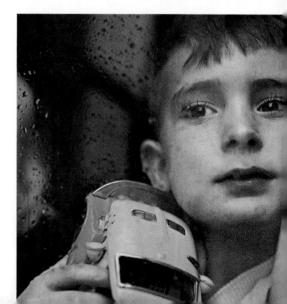

Mostly I'm happy

There's something I'm rarely
   without.
My supply of it doesn't run out.
I use it, yet there's more, and
   to spare.
It's something I like to share.
It's with me wherever I go.
What is it? Do you know?

                    My laugh!

I'm laughing. Why?
I'm just happy I am I!

Mother's here, home from the store.
She can come in—if I open the door!

                    Shall I?

I smile, though I feel quite shy.
I'll get to talking, by and by.

Daddy came to school.
He came to see:
my room,
my desk,
my pictures—
and me!

I'm happy, though I don't show it.
I feel nice inside, and I know it.
My laugh is tucked away just now.
But soon I'll smile. For Daddy knows how
to make dragons roar, goblins rumble,
and bears sort of mumble mumble
    mumble.

Especially for me

Ask me who I'd rather be.
The answer is easy—
I'd rather be ME!

My name may be Mary
or maybe it's Mike,
I can pack a knapsack
and go on a hike.
I can climb a tree.
I can ride a bike.

I can play with airplanes,
trucks and cars.
I can lie on my back
and look at the stars.

I can fish in a brook.
I can swim in a pool.
I can read a book.
I can use a tool.

There are lots of things
I can do and see.
So many things—
especially for me.

My friends

Friends share secrets (friends don't tell).
Friends share good times (and bad, as well).
Friends share things with one another.
That's because friends like each other.
Of all the happy things there are,
friends are the very best by far.

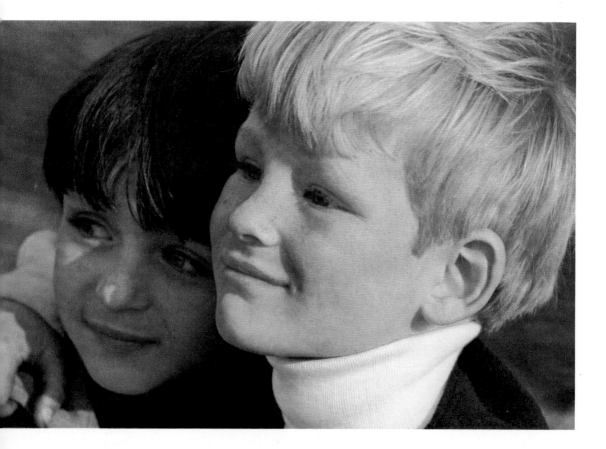

Which me?

I change from hour to hour and day to day
in such a surprising way
that sometimes I wonder which me is real
and if me-ness depends on how I feel.

Maybe as I grow
I'll know.

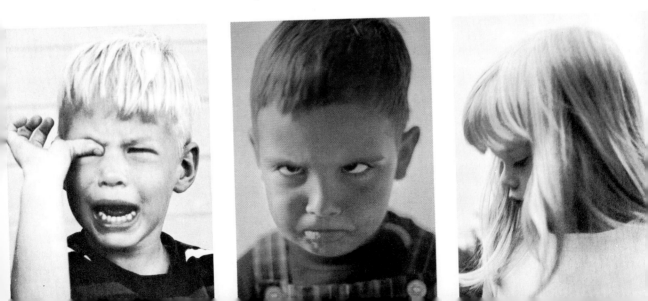

There's Nobody Exactly Like Me

It's my face

I don't think about my face very often, because I live behind it. But other people notice it. Sometimes they don't seem to believe I look like myself.

Grandma thinks I'm like her side of the family.

Mother says I'm like her. But Dad says he thinks I'll look like him when I grow up.

Uncle Bill says we have funny faces.

And everyone says my brother and I look as much alike as twins.

But my face doesn't really look exactly like anyone else's.

My eyes are blue. Mother's are brown.

I have freckles. Dad hasn't a one.

Grandma's face is kind. But she has wrinkles. I looked and looked, and I can't see one wrinkle on my face.

Uncle Bill is jolly and we laugh a lot together. Maybe when we're laughing we look a little alike. But not very much.

My brother does have freckles like mine, and blue eyes like mine. But his ears stick out more than mine do.

Maybe I look a little bit like Mother and Dad and Grandma and Uncle Bill and my brother. But no face anyplace is exactly like mine.

I think I look like ME.

Marks that are mine

If I press my finger on a window, I can see the fingerprint I leave there. No one in the world has fingerprints exactly like mine. And my footprints are different from everyone else's, too.

I look at my fingertips and I see many tiny lines. These lines form designs of loops and circles. Each finger has a different design. I have 10 fingers and 10 different fingerprints.

There might be somebody somewhere who looks almost like me. But that person's fingerprints would be different from mine.

In the hospital where I was born, there is a folder with my name on it. In the folder is a print of my foot. The other tiny babies in the hospital may have looked almost like me. But their footprints were different from mine.

Millions of children have tens of millions of fingerprints and footprints. But the marks made by my fingers and my feet are mine alone.

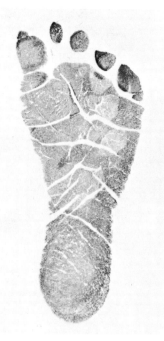

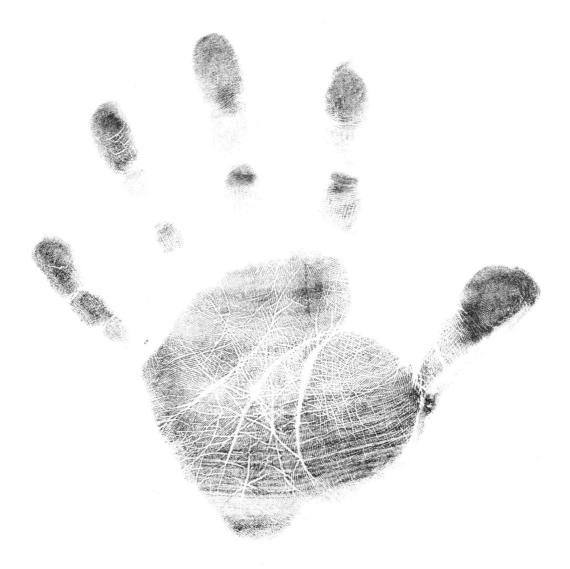

No one else has fingerprints,
handprints, or footprints
exactly like mine.

Look at my voice

No one's voice is exactly like mine. And my voice isn't always exactly the same. But people usually know me by my voice.

I use my lips, my tongue, and my teeth when I speak. I also use the soft part in the roof of my mouth and the muscles in my jaws, my nose, and my throat. These parts of me are different in some way from any other person's. And the way I use these parts is different from the way some other person uses his voice parts.

A special machine can print a picture of my voice. When I speak, the machine changes the sounds I make into lines that make a picture. Then the machine prints the picture on a piece of paper.

I can do many things with my voice to make it sound different. I can make it high. I can make it low. I can hold my nose or talk through a handkerchief. I can pretend that I am very old and make my voice shake. All of these things can make my voice picture look a little bit different.

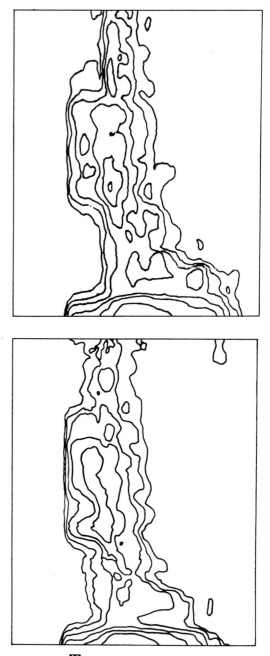

These are pictures of the same voice saying "you." The two pictures are alike in many ways.

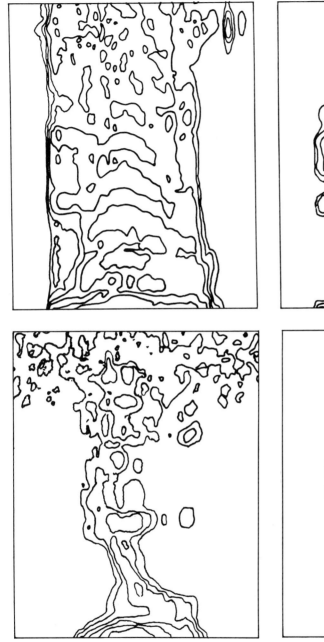
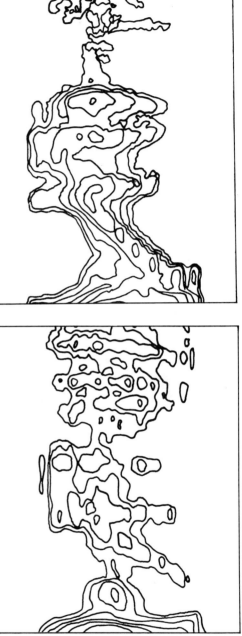

These are pictures of the voices of four people saying "you." Each picture is very different from the others.

Noses know me

Flowers smell sweet. Clean clothes smell clean. A dog smells doggy. A fish smells fishy. Everything has its own special scent. And so do I.

A bloodhound could find me if I were lost. My scent gets into my shoes and clothing. As I walk along, a little of my scent remains on the ground and on anything I touch. The bloodhound would follow me by smelling the ground and following my footsteps. He would follow my scent until he found me.

Because I have a special scent, I can send a letter to my cat when I am away from home. I wipe my face and hands with a paper tissue. I fold the tissue and put it in an envelope and mail it. My cat knows I sent the letter to her when she sniffs the tissue, because no one else has a scent exactly like mine.

Unmatched me

I look in a mirror and I see that the two sides of my face do not match.

One of my eyebrows is a little straighter than the other. One ear is set higher on the side of my head than my other ear. The two sides of my mouth do not match. One of my eyes is just a little bit bigger than the other. And no matter how hard I brush, one side of my hair stands up more than the other side.

Other parts of me don't exactly match, either. My right hand is larger than my left hand. My mother says her left hand is larger than her right.

When I get new shoes, one is always a bit tighter than the other. The man in the shoe store said that most people have one foot that is bigger than the other.

One of my legs is a tiny bit longer than the other leg. And one of my arms is a tiny bit longer than the other arm. I know this because the doctor told me so.

Why, if I could be divided into two parts the right side of me wouldn't exactly match the left side!

I'm not exactly like anyone else. Even the two halves of me are not exactly like each other.

I look in a mirror and I can see that the left half of my face is not exactly the same as the right half of my face.

If two left halves of my face were to grow side by side, the face I'd see would be somewhat different from the one I have.

And if two right halves of my face grew together, I'd see still another face. I'd rather have my unmatched face!

Messages for me

Every minute I'm awake my five senses send me messages. I see ten shades of green in the park. I hear a band and marching feet. I touch our baby's soft cheek. I smell the rain. I bite into a crisp red apple and I taste it.

The way I feel about these messages is special. I pay attention to the things I like best. No two people like and dislike exactly the same things. No two people ever receive exactly the same messages from their five senses.

Nobody else gets exactly the same messages that I do.

The things I do

I can do some things well.

I can write my name. It stands for me. And nobody else writes my name quite the way I do.

I can draw a picture. Even though other children are drawing the same thing, my picture will look different from theirs.

I can make our baby laugh out loud when I wiggle my ears. I can stand on my head—almost. I can dress myself and put my toys away. When it's dinnertime, I help set the table.

I'm proud of all the things I do well.

The secret me

The Secret Me is un-see-able.

The Secret Me lives in my brain and looks at the world through my eyes. The Secret Me thinks and dreams and plans and makes me act. Those thoughts and dreams and plans and actions are mine alone.

When I'm kind, or thoughtful, or honest, the Secret Me is happy. Being happy in this way helps me be the very best me I possibly can.

The Secret Me is truly me.

I will always be me

I was <u>me</u> when I was a baby. I am <u>me</u> now. And I will still be <u>me</u> when I grow up.

Some things about me are different than they were when I was a baby. My body is bigger and stronger than it was. I can do things now that I couldn't do when I was a baby. And I have learned lots of new things.

When I grow up, some things about me will be different than they are today. My body will grow even bigger and get even stronger. I will learn more, and I will be able to do even more things than I can do now.

But while I am growing, some things will stay the same. I will still have my family and friends and other special people in my life. I will still like many of the same things. I will still have my own thoughts and feelings. And I'll have my own special times to remember. All of these things are an important part of being me. So, even though I grow and change, I will still be me.

I'm human, and I have a human body. It's nice to know that I'm a little like all the other people in the world.

But my body is not exactly like anybody else's. The cells in my bones, in my muscles, in my brain, in all the parts of me, are like no other person's.

My face is mine alone.

My voice is not like anyone else's.

My fingerprints are my marks, and nobody else can make marks like them.

And there's more, because there's more to me than just my body. I'm special in other ways, too:

the way I alone think about
things;
the way only I feel about
things;
the things I myself think
important;
how I use my mind, my hands,
my special talents;

all together, these make me different from every other person in the world.

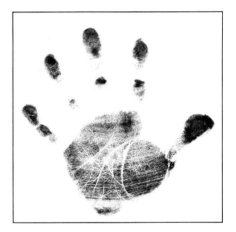

What does *Me* mean to Me?

I know some of the answer.

I know some ways in which I am different from every other person. But I don't know all the ways.

I'll have to think about it.

It might take a long, long time.

It might even take most of my life to find the answer.

It's worth thinking about, though.

While I'm figuring out more of the answer, I'll just be glad I'm me—exactly as I am.

New Words

Some of the words you have met in this book may be new to you. Many of them are words you'll meet again, so they are good words to know. Here are some of these words. Next to each word you are shown how to say it: **Achilles' tendon** (uh KIHL eez TEHN duhn). The part shown in capital letters is said a little more loudly than the rest of the word. Under each word, the meaning is given in a complete sentence.

Achilles' tendon (uh KIHL eez TEHN duhn)
The Achilles' tendon is a tough cord of tissue at the back of the ankle. It connects the calf muscles to the heel bone. The name comes from a Greek legend about the warrior, Achilles. When he was a baby, his mother dipped him in the River Styx so that he would live forever. But the heel she held him by did not get wet. So Achilles could be killed by a wound in the heel.

anvil (AN vuhl)
The anvil is one of three small bones (the others are the hammer and stirrup) in the middle ear. It is called the anvil because it is shaped like a blacksmith's anvil.

aorta (ay AWR tuh)
The aorta is the biggest and longest artery in the body. It carries fresh blood away from the heart.

appendix (uh PEHN dihks)
The appendix is a small, narrow baglike tube attached to the large intestine. So far as we know, it serves no purpose. But when it is infected, it causes a disease called appendicitis.

artery (AHR tuhr ee)
An artery is a tube that carries fresh blood away from the heart.

bacteria (bak TIHR ee uh)
Bacteria are tiny living cells. They can be seen only through a microscope.

biceps (BY sehps)
The large muscle in the front of the upper arm is called the biceps.

bladder (BLAD uhr)
The bladder is a stretchy baglike organ that stores urine until the body is ready to get rid of it.

bronchial tubes (BRAHNG kee uhl tyoobs)
Bronchial tubes lead from the trachea, or windpipe, to the lungs. The sickness called bronchitis is caused by an infection of the bronchial tubes.

calf (kaf)
The large muscle at the back of the leg, below the knee, is called the calf.

carbohydrate (KAHR boh HY drayt)
Carbohydrate is one of three main kinds of food (the others are protein and fat). Carbohydrates provide the energy to operate muscles and nerves. They also repair and build body tissues.

carbon dioxide (KAHR buhn dy AHK syd)
Carbon dioxide is the tasteless, odorless, colorless gas made by cells as they use food and oxygen.

cartilage (KAHR tuh lihj)
Cartilage is tough, strong tissue that is not as hard as bone. It is found between bones and in the nose and ears.

cochlea (KAHK lee uh)
The cochlea is a tube in the inner ear. It is shaped like the shell of a sea snail. Nerves in the cochlea send messages about sound to the brain.

collarbone (KAHL uhr bohn)
The long, thin, curved bone at the front of the shoulder is the collarbone.

cornea (KAWR nee uh)
The cornea is a clear cover over the colored part of the eyeball.

cytoplasm (SY tuh PLAZ uhm)
Everything in a cell except the nucleus is called cytoplasm.

dental hygienist (DEHN tuhl HY jee nihst)
A dental hygienist is a person who is trained to clean and polish teeth and assist the dentist in other ways.

dermis (DUR mihs)
The dermis is the layer of skin below the epidermis, which is the top layer.

diaphragm (DY uh fram)
The diaphragm is the large muscle between the lungs and the part of the body that contains the stomach and intestines. The diaphragm is used in breathing.

digestion (duh JEHS chuhn)
Digestion is the way in which food is changed in the body so that it can be used by the body.

enzyme (EN zime)
An enzyme is a special substance that helps digest food by breaking it down into tiny molecules.

epidermis (ehp uh DUR mihs)
The epidermis is the top layer of skin.

epiglottis (ehp uh GLAHT ihs)
The epiglottis is a kind of trap door made of cartilage that fits over the opening into the trachea, or windpipe. The epiglottis is open when air moves in and out of the trachea. When food is swallowed, the epiglottis closes to keep the food from entering the trachea.

esophagus (ee SAHF uh guhs)
The esophagus is the tube between the mouth and the stomach.

follicle (FAHL uh kuhl)
A follicle is an opening in the skin from which a hair grows.

gall bladder (gawl BLAD uhr)
The gall bladder is a small sack that lies beneath the liver. It stores liquids that help to digest food.

gene (jeen)
A gene is the tiny part of a cell that controls the color of hair, eyes, and skin; the height and shape of a person; and other important things.

gland (gland)
A gland is a part in the body that makes certain special things the body needs. There are sweat, tear, and oil glands. There are also glands that make liquids that help digest food and glands that control growth.

hammer (HAM uhr)
The hammer is one of three small bones (the others are the anvil and stirrup) in the middle ear. It is shaped like a hammer.

intestine (in TES tuhn)
The long, coiled tube that lies beneath the stomach is called the intestine. After food leaves the stomach, it enters the intestine, where the last part of digestion takes place.

iris (EYE rihs)
The iris is the blue, brown, gray, or green circle in the eye.

joint (joynt)
A joint is a point where bones fit together. Some joints move, like those in the legs. Other joints, like those at the top of the skull, do not move.

jugular vein (JUHG yuh luhr vayn)
The jugular vein is a large vein that carries blood from the head to the heart.

kidneys (KIHD neez)
Kidneys are two large organs behind the stomach that clean waste products from the blood.

kneecap (NEE kap)
The kneecap is the bone at the front of the knee joint.

laboratory (LAB ruh tawr ee)
A laboratory is a place where scientific work is done.

larynx (LAR ingks)
The larynx is a section of the air passage in the throat. It is between the back of the tongue and the trachea. It is sometimes called the voice box because it is shaped like a box and the upper part contains the vocal cords.

lens (lehns)
The lens is the part of the eye just behind the pupil. It sends light rays to the back of the eye.

liver (LIHV uhr)
The liver is a large gland that lies under the diaphragm. It makes a liquid that helps digest food. It does many other things as well. The liver stores fat, sugar, and iron. It helps blood to clot and destroys poisons.

lungs (lungz)
Lungs are two organs in the chest. Blood going back to the heart trades carbon dioxide for oxygen in the lungs.

melanin (MEHL uh nihn)
Bits of color found in skin, hair, and eyes are called melanin.

minerals (MIHN uhr uhlz)
Minerals are found in certain foods. The body needs minerals such as iron, calcium, and iodine to work properly.

molecule (MAHL uh kyool)
A molecule is the smallest bit into which something can be divided and still be the same as the original thing.

mucus (MYOO kuhs)
Mucus is a thick liquid found in the nose and other openings in the body.

nasal cavity (NAY zuhl KAV uh tee)
The nasal cavity is a large tunnel behind the nose.

navel (NAY vuhl)
The navel is the scar or mark in the middle of the stomach. It is sometimes called the bellybutton. This is where the umbilical cord was attached to a baby before birth.

nerve (nurv)
A nerve is a tiny cord along which messages travel to and from the brain.

nostrils (NAHS truhlz)
The nostrils are the two openings in the nose.

nucleus (NOO klee uhs)
The nucleus is the control center that directs the activities of a cell. It is usually near the middle of the cell.

optic nerve (AHP tihk nurv)
The nerve that leads from the back of the eyeball to the seeing part of the brain is called the optic nerve.

organ (AWR guhn)
An organ is a part of the body that does a special job. The heart is an organ. So are the lungs and brain.

orthodontist (awr thuh DAHN tihst)
An orthodontist is a special dentist who straightens teeth.

ovary (OH vuhr ee)
An ovary is one of two tiny glands in a girl's body. When a girl is grown, the ovaries will make the eggs from which babies can develop.

oxygen (AHK suh juhn)
Oxygen is a gas found in the air. Animals and plants need oxygen to live.

pancreas (PAN kree uhs)
The pancreas is a gland that makes a liquid that helps digest food.

pelvis (PEHL vihs)
The frame made by the hip bones and the end of the spine is the pelvis.

penis (PEE nihs)
The penis is the part of a boy's body that contains the urethra.

pituitary gland (pih TOO uh TEHR ee gland)
The pituitary gland controls the other glands. It lies just underneath the brain.

protein (PROH teen)
Protein is one of three main kinds of food (the others are carbohydrates and fats). Living things must have proteins to stay alive. The body needs proteins to build new cells and repair damaged ones.

protoplasm (PROH tuh PLAZ uhm)
The stuff that all living cells are made of is called protoplasm.

pulse (puhls)
The pulse is a beating caused by a stretching of the arteries after each heartbeat. It can be felt on the underside of the wrist and other places where an artery is near the surface.

pupil (PYOO puhl)
The pupil is a round opening through which light enters the eye. It looks like a black circle and is in the middle of the iris.

rectum (REHK tuhm)
The rectum is the lowest part of the large intestine. Solid waste products pass through it as they leave the body.

retina (REHT uh nuh)
The retina is the inner layer at the back of the eyeball. It contains thousands of nerves that carry messages to the optic nerve.

salivary glands (SAL uh vehr ee glanz)
Three pairs of glands, called salivary glands, make saliva. Saliva is a sticky liquid made in the mouth. It is important in the digestion of food.

scrotum (SKROH tuhm)
The scrotum is the part of a boy's body that contains the testicles.

shoulder blade (SHOHL duhr blayd)
The shoulder blade is the broad, flat bone at the back of the shoulder.

sinuses (SY nuhs uhz)
Sinuses are air cavities, or openings, in the skull joined to the nasal cavity.

sperm (spurm)
Sperm are cells that help a new life begin. Sperm cells are made in a man's testicles.

spinal cord (SPY nuhl kawrd)
The spinal cord is a long, thick bundle of nerves in the spine.

stirrup (STUR uhp)
The stirrup is one of three small bones (the others are the anvil and the hammer) in the middle ear. It looks like a stirrup.

tendon (TEHN duhn)
A tendon is a tough, strong cord
that joins a muscle and a bone.

testicles (TEHS tuh kuhlz)
Testicles are glands in a boy's scrotum.
When the boy is grown, the testicles
will make the sperm cells that make
the eggs in a woman's body develop
into a baby.

tissue (TISH oo)
Groups of cells that are alike and
work together to do special jobs for
the body are called tissue. There are
many kinds of tissue. Muscles are
tissue. Organs are made of many tissues.

tonsils (TAHN sulz)
Tonsils are a special tissue in the
throat that help the body fight germs.
But when the tonsils are badly
infected, they may almost block the
throat. Then they have to be taken out.

trachea (TRAY kee uh)
The trachea, or windpipe, is the tube
that carries air to the lungs. The
lower part of the trachea is connected
to the bronchial tubes.

triceps (TRY sehps)
The triceps is the large muscle at
the back of the upper arm.

umbilical cord (uhm BIHL uh kuhl kawrd)
The umbilical cord is the cord that
joins a baby to its mother before
birth. A baby receives food and
oxygen through this cord. After a
baby is born, this cord is cut. The
scar or mark that is left is called
the navel.

ureters (yu REE tuhrz)
Ureters are the tubes that lead
from the kidneys to the bladder.

urethra (yu REE thruh)
The urethra is the tube that leads
from the bladder out of the body.
It carries liquid waste products the
body cannot use.

urine (YUR uhn)
Urine is the liquid waste product
made by the kidneys.

uterus (YOO tuhr uhs)
The uterus is the organ in a mother's
body where a baby can grow and wait
to be born.

vagina (vuh JY nuh)
The vagina is the part of a girl's
body that leads from the uterus out
of the body.

veins (vaynz)
Veins are tubes in the body that
carry used blood back to the heart.

vena cava (VEE nuh KAY vuh)
A vena cava is either of two large
veins that open into the heart.

vitamin (VY tuh mihn)
A vitamin is an important substance
that the body needs to stay healthy.
There are many different kinds of
vitamins. Milk, meat, fish, vegetables,
fruit, eggs, and cereal contain vitamins.

vocal cords (VOH kuhl kawrds)
The vocal cords are two strips of tissue
that stretch across the larynx. Air
passing through the larynx vibrates the
vocal cords and makes sounds.

waste products (wayst PRAHD uhktz)
Things the body cannot use are called
waste products. Liquid waste is
passed out through the urethra. Solid
waste is passed out of the body
through the rectum.

Illustration acknowledgments

The publishers of *Childcraft* gratefully acknowledge the following artists, photographers, publishers, agencies, and corporations for illustrations in this volume. Page numbers refer to two-page spreads. The words *"(left)," "(center)," "(top)," "(bottom),"* and *"(right)"* indicate position on the spread. All illustrations are the exclusive property of the publishers of *Childcraft* unless names are marked with an asterisk (*).

1: Robert Keys
4-5: © Peter Fronk, Click/Chicago *
6-7: *Childcraft* photo, courtesy William Ogden School
8-9: *Childcraft* photo, courtesy William Ogden School
10-11: © Bob Rashid, Click/Chicago *
12-13: © Lee Balterman, Gartman Agency *
14-15: *Childcraft* photo
16-17: © Steve Leonard *
18-21: *Childcraft* photos
22-23: *(left) Childcraft* diagram; *(top right) Childcraft* photos, *(bottom right)* Phoebe Dunn *
24-25: *Childcraft* photos
26-27: Bob S. Smith, Rapho Guillumette *
28-29: Chuck Wood
30-31: *(left)* International Society for Educational Information, Tokyo, Inc.; *(bottom, center, and right) Childcraft* photos
32-33: Tom Mosier, Terra
34-47: *Childcraft* diagrams
48-49: *(left) Childcraft* photo by Joel Cole, Rush-Presbyterian-St. Luke's Medical Center, Chicago; *(right)* Product Illustration, Inc.
50-51: © David R. Frazier Photolibrary *
52-53: *Childcraft* photo, courtesy A. J. Nystrom & Co. and *Childcraft* diagrams
54-55: *Childcraft* photo by Don Ornitz; Diagrams, *Childcraft* art
56-59: *Childcraft* diagrams
60-61: © Arthur Sirdofsky, Medichrome *
62-63: *(top) Childcraft* photo; *(bottom)* Phoebe Dunn *
64-65: *Childcraft* photos
66-67: *Childcraft* diagram
68-69: *(left)* © Lawrence Migdale *; *(right) Childcraft* photo
70-71: *Childcraft* photo and diagrams
72-73: *Childcraft* photo and diagram
74-75: *Childcraft* photo
76-77: *Childcraft* photo and diagrams
78-79: *(left) Childcraft* photos; *(right) Childcraft* photos by Ed Reif
80-81: *Childcraft* diagrams
82-83: © Eunice Harris, Photo Researchers *
84-85: *Childcraft* photos and diagrams
86-87: *Childcraft* diagrams and *Childcraft* photo by Phoebe Dunn
88-91: *Childcraft* photos
92-93: *(top left) Childcraft* photo; *(top right and bottom left) Childcraft* photos by Phoebe Dunn; *(bottom right)* Phoebe Dunn *
94-95: © Lawrence Manning, Click/Chicago *
96-97: *Childcraft* diagrams
98-99: *Childcraft* diagrams; Robert Demarest
100-101: Mike Fisher, Custom Medical *
102-103: Mike Fisher, Custom Medical *
104-105: *(left)* Phoebe Dunn *; *(top right)* © John Moss, The Stock Shop *; *(bottom right)* © Custom Medical *
106-107: *Childcraft* photos
108-109: © Steve Leonard *
110-111: *(left)* Coleman Co. *; *(right) Childcraft* photos by Arthur Shay, Phoebe Dunn *
112-113: © David Frazier Photolibrary *
114-115: Marilou Wise
116-117: *(top left)* Marc and Evelyne Bernheim, Rapho Guillumette *; *(bottom left)* John LaDue *; *(top right)* John LaDue *;
Marc and Evelyne Bernheim, Rapho Guillumette *; *(bottom right)* Artstreet *
118-119: *(top left)* John LaDue *; *(bottom left) Childcraft* photo; *(top right) Childcraft* photo; *(center right)* Fritz Henle, Photo Researchers *; *(bottom right)* John LaDue *
120-121: *(left)* Richard Harrington, Miller Services *; *(top right)* Miller Services *; *(bottom right)* Richard Harrington, Miller Services *, John LaDue *
122-123: *(left)* Madeline Hobbs, Tom Stack & Associates *; *(right)* Bob S. Smith, Rapho Guillumette *
124-125: *(top)* Vivienne *; *(bottom left)* Christa Armstrong, Rapho Guillumette *; *(bottom right) Childcraft* photo by Ray Halin
126-127: *(left)* © M. Serraillier, Photo Researchers *; *(right)* John LaDue *
128-129: © Steve Leonard *
130-131: *Childcraft* photos by Phoebe Dunn
132-133: *Childcraft* photos
134-135: Phoebe Dunn *
136-137: *Childcraft* photos
138-139: Lawrence Migdale
140-141: *Childcraft* photos by James Annan
142-143: *(left)* Jim Collins *; *(top right) Childcraft* photo, *(bottom right)* Bob Smith, Rapho Guillumette *
144-147: *Childcraft* photo
148-149: Denver Gillen
150-151: *(left, top to bottom) Childcraft* photos; *(right, top to bottom) Childcraft* photo; *Childcraft* photo by Phoebe Dunn *; © Dan McCoy *
152-153: © Steve Leonard
154-155: *Childcraft* photo and diagram
156-157: *(left)* Shriners Hospital for Crippled Children, Chicago *; *(right)* from *Growth and Development of Children* by E. H. Watson and G. H. Lowrey, © 1967 Year Book Medical Publishers *
158-159: Marilou Wise
160-161: *Childcraft* photo and diagram
162-163: © Robert Frerck *
164-165: *Childcraft* photos
166-171: © Robert Frerck *
172-173: © Robert Frerck *; Camerique *
174-175: *(left)* George W. Lange, D.D.S. *; *(right) Childcraft* photo
176-181: © Robert Frerck *
182-183: © Bob Rashid, Click/Chicago *
184-185: *Childcraft* photos
186-187: *(top)* Phoebe Dunn *; *(center and right) Childcraft* photos
188-189: *(top)* Bonnie Freer *; *(bottom)* Rhodes Patterson *
190-191: *(top)* © Lawrence Migdale *; *(bottom) Childcraft* photo
192-193: *(left)* Walter Chandoha *; *(right)* Yerkes Regional Primate Research Center *
194-195: *Childcraft* photo
196-197: © Steve Leonard *
198-199: *(left) Childcraft* diagram; *(right) Childcraft* photo by Carol Ann Bales
202-203: United Artists Studios
204-205: *(left)* Victoria Beller-Smith; *(top right)* © Lawrence Migdale *; *(bottom right)* © E. R. Degginger *
206-207: © Robert Frerck *
208-209: © Victoria Beller-Smith
210-211: *Childcraft* photos

212-213: © Steve Leonard *
214-215: *(left) Childcraft* photos; *(right)* © David R. Frazier Photolibrary *
216-219: *Childcraft* photos
220-221: *(top)* Phoebe Dunn *; *(center)* Shankar's International Children's Competition, New Delhi, India *; *(bottom) Childcraft* photo
222-223: Phoebe Dunn *
224-225: *(top and bottom left) Childcraft* photos; *(bottom right)* Shankar's International Children's Competition, New Delhi, India *
226-227: *Childcraft* photos
228-229: *(top) Childcraft* photo; *(center)* Shankar's International Children's Competition, New Delhi, India *; *(bottom) Childcraft* photo, courtesy Three Worlds
230-231: *(top)* International Photo-Art Service *; *(bottom) Childcraft* photo
232-233: © Steve Leonard *
234-235: *(top left)* Charles Vallone *; *(bottom left)* Delores Lawler from Tom Stack & Associates *; *(top right)* Fred Lyon, Rapho Guillumette *, Vivienne *; *(center right) Childcraft* photo; *(bottom right)* Michael Mauney, Black Star *
236-237: *(left)* H. Armstrong Roberts *; *(top right)* Claude Chamberland, 1968 Newspaper National Snapshot Awards *; *(bottom right)* Stock Photos Unlimited *
238-239: *(top left)* Stock Photos Unlimited *; *(bottom left)* Vivienne *; *(top right)* Wayne Miller, Magnum *; *(center right)* International Photo-Art Service *; *(bottom right)* Phoebe Dunn *
240-241: *(left)* Bonnie Freer *; *(right)* Dan Morrill, Stock Photo Finders *
242-243: *(left)* Arizona Photographic Associates, Inc. *; *(top right)* Jean-Claude LeJeune, Tom Stack & Associates *, *(center right) Childcraft* photo, *(bottom right)* H. Armstrong Roberts *
244-245: *(top left)* Lee Balterman *, *(center left) Childcraft* photo; *(bottom left)* International Photo-Art Service *; *(top right)* Myrl A. Garas, Tom Stack & Associates *, *(center right)* Lee Balterman *, *(bottom right)* Declan Haun, Black Star *
246-247: *(top left)* Gerry Souter *, *(bottom left)* Declan Haun, Black Star *; *(right) Childcraft* photos
248-249: *(top left)* Vivienne *; *(bottom left) Childcraft* photo; *(right)* Wayne Miller, Magnum *
250-251: *(left)* Bonnie Freer *; *(top right)* H. Armstrong Roberts *; *(bottom right)* Arizona Photographic Associates, Inc. *
252-253: *(top left)* Ken Short *; *(center left)* Bonnie Freer *; *(bottom left) Childcraft* photo, Phoebe Dunn *; *(right)* Arizona Photographic Associates, Inc.*, Stock Photos Unlimited *, Vivienne *
254-255: © Steve Leonard *
256-257: © Peter Fronk, Click/Chicago *
258-259: *Childcraft* photos
260-261: Voiceprint Laboratories, Division of Farrington Mfg. Co. *
262-263: Walter Chandoha *
264-265: *Childcraft* photos
266-267: Phoebe Dunn *
268-269: *(top left)* Phoebe Dunn *; *(bottom left)* Charles Vallone *; *(right)* Phoebe Dunn *
270-271: © Liane Enkelis/Stock, Boston *
272-273: *(left) Childcraft* photo and diagram; *(right) Childcraft* photos except *(top left)* Myrl A. Garas, Tom Stack & Associates *
274-275: *Childcraft* photo by Don Ornitz, Globe

Cover: Beverly Pardee

Index

This index is an alphabetical list of the important topics covered in this book. It will help you find information given in both words *and* pictures. To help you understand what an entry means, there is often a helping word in parentheses. For example, **cornea** (eye). If there is information in both words and pictures, you will see the words *with pictures* after the page number. If there is *only* a picture, you will see the word *picture* before the page number. If you do not find what you want in this index, please go to the General Index in Volume 15, which is a key to all of the books.